DEAN BRETTSCHNEIDER is a professional baker and patissier. He began his career at the age of 16 as an apprentice at the award-winning Rangiora Bakery, in a small rural North Canterbury township. In 1988 he won the New Zealand Apprentice of the Year for Baking and Pastry Cooking and captained the victorious New Zealand Baking Training Centre Apprentice Baking Team in the Trans Tasman Baking Competitions in Melbourne.

He worked in the USA, Britain and Europe after completing his apprenticeship, gaining experience in all areas of the baking and patisserie trade, including work in exclusive hotels, supermarket in-store bakeries and alongside some of Europe's leading bakers and pastry chefs. On his return to New Zealand, he was employed on Ernest Adams' research and development team, and attended the American Institute of Baking in Kansas, USA. He then moved on to teach at the New Zealand Baking Training Centre in Christchurch, and two years later bought a small craft bakery, Windsor Cakes, in Dunedin.

Always the competitor, Dean entered and won many awards at the annual New Zealand Baking Society competitions and joined the executive of the society as their youngest member. After three years of running his own business, Dean moved to Auckland to join Goodman Fielder Milling and Baking, heading up Champion's technical support department, where he assists Champion customers with problem solving, and supplies staff training and product development. He travels to major bakery expositions throughout the world to ensure that Champion is up to date with all the latest innovations and bakery trends.

Dean regularly writes articles for the *New Zealand Bakers Journal*; gives presentations and demonstrations in New Zealand, Australia and the USA; judges the New Zealand Baker of the Year Competition; and moderates all bakery Trade Certificate Examinations in New Zealand. His philosophy for successful baking is 'commitment, dedication and passion combined with a little fun'.

He lives in Auckland with his wife Susan and their young son, Jason. This is his first book.

LAURAINE JACOBS is an award-winning senior feature writer and restaurant reviewer for *Cuisine* magazine. She trained at the London Cordon Bleu School of Cookery where she passed the Advanced Certificate of Cookery and is one of only four New Zealanders to have been awarded the prestigious Certified Culinary Professional designation from the International Association of Culinary Professionals.

Lauraine was a principal of Austin's Cooking School and regularly gives cooking classes at Auckland's Epicurean Workshop and other cooking schools in New Zealand. She travels frequently to the USA where she is on the executive board of the IACP, and has spoken at workshops at several international conferences.

She lives in Auckland with her husband Murray and their university student son Scott, and lists her hobbies as golf, food and wine, and e-mailing daughter Katie who has flown the coop to New York. This is her second book for Tandem Press, the first being the award-winning *New Taste, New Zealand*.

the New Zealand baker

Dean Brettschneider and
Lauraine Jacobs

Photographs by
Kieran Scott

TANDEM PRESS

First published in New Zealand in 1999 by
Tandem Press
2 Rugby Road
Birkenhead, Auckland 10
New Zealand

ISBN 1 877178 55 1

Cover and text design by Christine Hansen
Produced by M & F Whild Typesetting Services, Auckland
Printed in Hong Kong by South China Printing Company

ACKNOWLEDGEMENTS

Without the support of Goodman Fielder Milling and Baking NZ Limited this book would have remained a dream. The Goodman Fielder Technical Training Centre has been used for all the recipe development and testing, and the endless supply of Champion and Elfin flour products has been much appreciated. Dean has been generously allowed the time, often snatched at all hours between his technical advising, to write and format the recipes for the book. We are very grateful to the management for their confidence and support of this project. Thanks also to Fiona Branson for her patient test bakery work.

We are also grateful to Fisher and Paykel NZ Limited for supplying their latest domestic oven for all test baking and recipe testing.

We would like to thank all the professional bakers and chefs from around New Zealand for their generosity in sharing their recipes, and for the time spent with us as we gathered information and asked endless questions.

Susan Brettschneider has been very supportive, proofing Dean's writing, and understanding the late nights and early starts, and holding the home together through frequent absences.

The Epicurean Workshop, Newmarket, and Milly's Kitchen Shop, Ponsonby, have supplied specialist kitchenware and baking equipment, and we are very grateful for the generous use of The Epicurean's cooking school for photography of the baking equipment.

We are indebted to Tandem Press and all the team who have been associated with the book and its production: Kieran Scott for his brilliant photography, Bob Ross and Helen Benton for their guidance, Sara Haddad for production, Alison Mudford for editing, and designer Christine Hansen for her excellent, appealing layout and design.

—*Dean Brettschneider and Lauraine Jacobs, 1999*

CONTENTS

Introduction   9
The Ingredients   10
The Equipment   23
Formulas and Measurements   30
All About Bread   34
All About Cakes, Sponges & Biscuits   43
All About Pastries   49
Bordeaux Bakery   58
City Cake Company   66
Copenhagen Bakery   72
Dean Brettschneider   78
Dixon Street Deli   86
Dovedale Foods   92
Heavens' Bakery   96
Hillyers of Lincoln   100
Janus Bakkerij   104
Muffin Time   110
Nada Bakery   114
Pandoro Bakery   118
Rembrandts   134
Rocket Kitchen   142
Sydenham Bakery   148
Under the Red Verandah   154
Vinnies Restraurant   158
Sources   162
Bibliography   163
Index   164

INTRODUCTION

'BREAD IS THE STAFF OF LIFE.'

New Zealanders have always been champions of baking – whether in large commercial bakeries churning out loaves by the thousands, the small village bakery turning out just enough bread and cakes for the local community, or the keen housewife baking to fill empty tins and empty tummies. There's nothing more satisfying than the aroma of freshly baked bread, or the knowledge that there is a rich, moist cake waiting to be cut into.

Right from the days of the first settlers, bread has been a very important, indeed staple item, in the national diet. New Zealand, like most of the western world, has been heavily influenced by the traditional European baker, with his flair for producing a variety of breads, wholesome cakes and dainty pastries. The professional baking industry has relied on a continual influx of mainly Dutch and German bakers to lead the way, and right up to the end of the nineties it has been these people who have dominated professional baking in New Zealand.

Great baking requires painstaking care, knowledge of technique and procedures, and a great deal of passion and commitment. Recent directions in baking are leading bakers around the world back to their baking roots. The artisan style of baking, reflecting passion and interest inspired by the feel of the dough, has sparked a return to the smaller, more personal bakery with a highly individual touch.

Another big influence on baking has been the shift from tea to coffee in our diet and the rise of the café culture. Social gatherings over a cup of coffee, accompanied by a baking 'treat' have become a daily ritual in our lives. Bakeries, recognising this trend, have met the market by installing comfortable seating, coffee machines and producing tasty cakes and pastries to accompany the coffee they serve.

This book was inspired by such bakers – true professionals who produce top quality baking for an apprentice audience. We combed the country, seeking the classical, the innovative and the passionate bakers who would share their recipes with other professional bakers and the sophisticated home baker. A real cross section of regional bakers, leaders in the industry, and influences from the great bakers of Europe are included, along with some of the smart new business-driven and artisan-style bakers. We are very grateful to them for generously sharing these recipes and their time. Dean Brettschneider, co-author, has meticulously tested and adapted these professionals' recipes, and shares his vast knowledge and understanding of baking in the book's comprehensive reference section. Dean holds the position of technical support manager for the baking industry at Goodman Fielder's milling and baking division. In this capacity he assists, advises and counsels bakers throughout New Zealand and is frequently invited to speak at conferences throughout the world.

HOW TO USE THIS BOOK

The first part of this book has been carefully written with information on every aspect of baking. There are several comprehensive sections: All About Bread, All About Cakes, All About Pastries, and lots of information about ingredients, measurements and much more. Before attempting the recipes in this book take the time to read through these notes. In order to be a successful baker it is important to understand and appreciate the background information, the processes and the reasons for following baking formulas. Baking, while a real art, is an exact science with no room for improvisation and error.

The recipes are all set out in measurements and should be measured in the exact quantities given, or can be scaled up in direct proportion. Use scales to weigh all ingredients, and if purchasing scales, seek out a set that has increments of one gram or two grams for accuracy. There are charts included that identify faults that commonly occur, and we hope that bakers will find these useful, if anything seems imperfect.

These recipes have all been adapted from the bakeries who supplied them. We hope that bakers throughout New Zealand will use and enjoy this professional fare, and spend many long, satisfying hours baking.

THE INGREDIENTS

WHEAT FLOUR

Wheat flour is the most important ingredient in the bakery. It provides bulk and structure to most of the baker's products, including breads, cakes, biscuits and pastries. There are many different types and each has been designed for a specific reason or with a finished end product in mind.

Flour is obtained from the cereal wheat. A grain of wheat consists of six main parts, but the endosperm, bran and the germ are the most important:

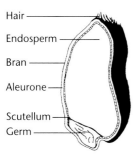

1. Endosperm, 85 percent: is the white part of the wheat grain from which white flour is milled once the bran and germ have been removed.

    It largely consists of:
    - tightly packed starch granules
    - soluble proteins (albumens)
    - insoluble gluten forming proteins (glutenin and gliadin)
    - oil
    - moisture
    - mineral matter

2. Bran, 13 percent: is the outside skin of the wheat grain and consists of six different principal layers, ranging from protective layers to colouring and enzyme active layers. During the milling of white flour the bran layers are mostly removed. The bran is blended back in with the finely ground endosperm (white flour) to produce wheatmeal or brown flour.

3. Germ, 2 percent: is located inside the wheat grain and is the embryo from which wheat can reproduce itself. It is mostly removed in the milling of white flour because the oil soon becomes rancid and the enzymes have a detrimental influence on the fermentation process in bread making.

    The germ is rich in:
    - oil
    - calcium
    - vitamin B (thiamine, riboflavine and nicotinic acid)
    - enzymes (diastatic and proteolytic)

The germ is blended back into the endosperm and bran to produce wholemeal flour.

Milling Wheat

There are two styles of flour milling still being done in New Zealand: stone milling and roller milling, the latter being the most popular for flour quality and profitability.

The stone milling method was used in the Middle Ages to produce a meal from which a loaf of bread could be made. The system consisted of two large grooved stones placed one on top of the other. The bottom one remained stationary while the top one revolved. Grain was fed into the centre of the two stones and gradually crushed to a coarse meal. Generally this mechanism was powered by man, donkey, or in latter years, by water wheel or windmill. Today, authentic stone milled flour is produced by mechanised methods.

Roller milling is more specialised and sophisticated and involves gradual reduction. The wheat grain goes through many different processes to achieve top quality flour, for example:

- cleaning – the grains are checked for foreign matter and screened
- conditioning – this softens the endosperm and toughens the bran layers
- break rolls – fluted rollers fracture and split apart the grain (many times)
- sifters – sieve and separate the bran, endosperm (semolina) and germ
- reduction rolls – smooth rollers crush the endosperm further to finally produce flour
- packaging – flour placed into bag or bulk tankers
- flour testing – flour undergoes many analytical tests to ensure quality
- test baking – flour undergoes test baking

Composition of Flour

The composition of flour will naturally be similar to that of the wheat from which it is milled. An average composition would be:

STRONG FLOUR %	CONSTITUENTS	SOFT FLOUR %
70	Starch	72
11–13	Insoluble gluten forming proteins	7–8
13–15	Moisture	13–15
2.5	Sugar	2.5
1–1.5	Fat	1–1.5
1	Soluble proteins	1
0.5	Mineral salts	0.5

Extraction Rate

This term refers to the amount of flour that is obtained from the wheat after milling, for example, if the flour miller obtains 78 kg of white flour from 100 kg of wheat, the extraction rate equals 78 percent. The extraction rate for wholemeal flour is 100 percent and for pastry flours it is between 55 percent and 65 percent (given that you require a cleaner, whiter speck-free flour for the manufacture of pastry products).

Insoluble Gluten-Forming Proteins

The insoluble proteins present in flour are known as gluten. Gluten is made up of two proteins called glutenin and gliadin, both having different characteristics: glutenin producing elastic properties and gliadin producing extensible properties. Gluten is produced in a bread dough, for example, when water has been added and the dough has been mixed sufficiently to develop the gluten. The suitability of a flour for bakery products is determined by the quality of the gluten and in some cases the quantity it contains. Flour that contains good quality gluten is known as strong flour; flour that contains low quality gluten is known as soft flour.

Storage of Flour

Flour and meals should be stored under the following conditions to prevent deterioration:

- Temperature: 10–16°C
- Environment: dry conditions
- Time:
  White flours 3–6 months
  Wholemeal and brown flours 3–4 months
  Meals and grains 2–3 months

Always ensure that stock rotation is adhered to: F.I.F.O. (first in, first out).

Hand Test for Flour Strength

The strength of the flour can be identified by squeezing it in the hand. A weak/soft flour will cling and clump together and feels very smooth when the hand is opened, whereas a strong flour will crumble again to a powder and feel slightly coarse when rubbed between the fingers.

Types of Flour

A wide variety of flour is milled from wheat and other grains.

Strong flour (Champion High Grade and Elfin High Grade) contains a high level of protein (gluten) which is beneficial for the manufacture of bread, yeast-raised varieties and puff pastry. Heavy fruit cakes are sometimes made using strong flours.

Medium flour has been milled to provide medium strength for use in such goods as short pastry products, powder aerated goods (scones, light fruit cakes, muffins, biscuits and slices).

Soft flour (Champion Standard Plain and Elfin Plain Flour) has a low protein (gluten) content and is ideal for making cakes, sponges and some biscuits.

Pastry flour has been milled from the centre of the wheat, giving a cleaner, whiter speck-free flour which is ideal for the manufacture of pastry products that require refrigeration or freezing in their raw state. The protein (gluten) level is of medium quality; however, since it is milled from the centre of the wheat grain it is of very good quality with excellent extensibility properties. This flour is mainly used by commercial pastry manufacturers for top quality pies, pastries, sausage rolls, etc.

High ratio flour (special cake flour) is milled to a very fine particle size and heavily bleached, a treatment that increases its moisture absorbing properties and makes it an ideal flour for cakes and sponges that contain a high level of sugar and liquids to the quantity of flour, thus increasing the shelf life. This flour is mainly used in commercial bakeries.

Self rising flour (Champion Self Rising and Elfin Self Rising Flour) is usually a medium strength flour into which has been blended a proportion of baking powder at the rate of approximately two percent of the flour. It is used for batters, scones, pikelets, etc. This product is mainly used when the weighing of baking powder is difficult due to the small amount required.

Wholemeal flour is milled from the whole wheat grain and therefore contains the bran and germ. It is suitable for all bread and yeast-raised products, pastries, cakes and biscuits. When using wholemeal flour in a recipe, consideration should be given to the obviously high amount of bran the flour contains. Bran acts like tiny pieces of glass within an unbaked product, cutting and damaging the gluten (protein) network that has been developed in order to give strength, structure and volume to the finished baked product. In most cases the addition of extra dried gluten or strong flour is necessary to compensate.

Semolina flour is simply coarsely ground endosperm and can be used for thickening pie fillings, dusting the baker's peel for ease of transferring the breads onto the oven's hearth, and as an ingredient in crusty bread formulations.

Rye flour is the next most popular flour for bread making, after white and wholemeal, and is milled from the cereal rye. Milling of the rye grain is done in the same manner as for the wheat grain. Although rye flour contains some flour proteins, they do not form gluten. Therefore, breads made with 100 percent rye flour will be sticky at the dough stage and heavy and dense after baking. It is common practice to use a percentage of white strong flour when making rye breads, at a ratio of 25–40 percent rye flour and 60–75 percent white strong flour. Rye flour is available as either light rye or dark rye and is commonly used for dusting breads prior to baking.

Rye meal is produced by grinding the entire rye grain. It is coarse and dark and mainly used for pumpernickel bread and rolls.

Gluten flour is simply dried protein (gluten) from within wheat flour. Flour milled in New Zealand is of excellent quality and the addition of dried gluten is only necessary when excessive amounts of enriching and softening products (fats, sugar, grains and excessive liquids) are used within a recipe.

Cornflour is obtained from the cereal maize. It is almost 100 percent starch and does not contain any insoluble gluten-forming proteins. Cornflour is mainly used as a thickening agent for custards, sauces and fillings. It can also be used to dilute strong flours when short, tender eating qualities are required, for example, in shortbread.

Rice flour is obtained from the cereal rice. It is almost 100 percent starch and does not contain any insoluble gluten-forming proteins. Rice flour is added to cake recipes and biscuits to assist with absorbing the liquids for either keeping qualities or crispness properties, for example, in shortbread.

Soya flour is obtained from the soya bean and is very rich in protein but does not contain any insoluble gluten-forming proteins. It is very high in fat, making it an excellent ingredient for any bread recipe that requires keeping qualities, even texture and increased volume.

Malt flour and malt products are obtained from barley and wheat that have undergone a controlled process known as malting. This begins after the grains have been cleaned. Germination then takes place in an environment that has been controlled by temperature and humidity. During this period, the starch within the grain is converted into simple sugars. This is then halted when the grains are subjected to heat during the drying stages. Malt products are an important food source for yeast in yeast-raised doughs and the following improvements are to be expected if used:

- volume
- texture
- colour
- flavour
- eating qualities
- increased shelf life

Organic flour is milled from organically grown wheat. This wheat is grown by selected farmers and not cross-contaminated with wheat that is treated with chemical sprays, etc. Commercial flour mills are unable to process organic grains in conjunction with other grains, therefore organic flour is produced in dedicated mills. Most baked products can be made using organic flours. Quality is sometimes variable and yields are usually lower, therefore a premium price is charged.

SALT

Salt is a natural mineral. New Zealand salt is made at Lake Grasmere, near Blenheim. It comes in many different forms: table salt, sea salt, iodised salt, vacuum salt and rock salt (the latter mainly used for decoration due to its large crystal size). The chemical name is *sodium chloride*.

Salt plays a very important role in baking. More than just a flavour or seasoning enhancer, it also has these functions:

- strengthens the gluten structure and makes it more stretchable
- controls the rate of fermentation within yeast-raised doughs
- enhances the flavour and eating qualities
- improves the crust and crumb colour and stability
- increases the shelf life

Salt is hygroscopic and should be stored away from moisture.

SUGAR

By the term 'sugar' we mean sucrose which is obtained from two sources: cane and beet sugar. They are natural substances and belong to the chemical group of carbohydrates. Once refining of sugar has been completed, it can be categorised into two divisions: grains and syrups.

Grains

- caster sugar – fine crystals
- granulated sugar – coarse crystals
- nib sugar – large crystals (similar to rock salt in size)
- cube sugar
- brown sugar – soft and coarse
- raw sugar
- icing sugar – granulated sugar crushed to a powder, with starch added

Syrups

- golden syrup
- treacle
- honey
- glucose
- molasses

Sugar and syrups possess the following properties:

- sweetness and flavour
- creates tenderness and fineness of texture by weakening the gluten structure (shortens)
- caramelises during baking and gives crust colour
- acts as source of food for yeast during fermentation
- improves shelf life by retaining moisture
- acts as a creaming agent with fats, and as a foaming agent with eggs

Sugar is also hygroscopic and should be stored away from any moisture.

EGGS

An average fresh egg composition is as follows:

	WHOLE EGGS %	WHITES %	YOLKS %
Water	73	86	49
Protein	13	12	17
Fat	12	–	32
Minerals	2	2	2

The types of eggs used in bakeries include:

- shell eggs
- chilled liquid egg pulp
- frozen liquid pulp
- frozen egg white
- dried egg white

Note: egg whites are known as albumen.

Eggs possess the following properties when used in bakery products.

(i) Moisturising: eggs contain 73 percent water and have the ability to moisturise their own weight in flour.

(ii) Aeration: whisked eggs can incorporate air and increase volume in such products as meringues and sponges.

(iii) Structural: when eggs are subjected to heat during the baking process, they expand, the proteins coagulate (set) and the structure is established.

(iv) Emulsifying: the egg yolk contains a natural emulsifying agent known as lecithin. The lecithin assists in combining two substances or ingredients that normally do not mix well – water and fat.

(v) Enriching: eggs contain high levels of protein and fat which add to the nutritional value of the baked product.

(vi) Flavouring: eggs have their own distinctive flavour.

(vii) Colouring: eggs give bakery products a yellow tinge.

(viii) Glazing: when eggs are mixed with the appropriate amount of water or milk, they can be used to glaze the surface of many bakery products.

(ix) Eating quality: eggs give lightness, moistness and flavour to baked products.

(x) Keeping qualities: the moisturising, emulsifying, enriching and general softening properties of the egg will assist in extending the shelf life of baked products.

All fresh eggs should be stored in a cool place (preferably in a refrigerator) and be used within three to four weeks of purchase.

The average weight (excluding the shell) of a: size 5 egg is 40 g

size 6 egg is 45 g

size 7 egg is 50 g

Weighing eggs is not difficult. Lightly beat eggs in a cup or small bowl, then pour into your weighing container. Any left over egg can be stored in the freezer in an air tight container until needed.

MILK AND MILK PRODUCTS

Whole milk is fresh milk as it comes from the cow, with nothing added or removed. It contains 3.5 percent fat (known as milk fat), 8.5 percent nonfat milk solids and 88 percent water. Milk adds the following characteristics to bakery products:

- moistness
- texture
- colour
- eating qualities
- shelf life
- nutrition

Milk also comes in other forms:

Milk powder is whole or skim milk that has been dried to a powder. Both can be reconstituted with water. Milk powders are often used in bread recipes to add richness and assist as a food source for yeast. It will also add crust colour. Store in a cool dry place.

Condensed milk is whole milk that has been heat treated and has had approximately 60 percent of its water removed before adding sugar at a concentration of 42–45 percent. It is then packed into sterile containers. Condensed milk is used as an enriching or sweetening agent, for example, in caramel filling. Once opened, cover and store in a cool place. The high sugar content acts as a preservative.

Evaporated milk is milk, either whole or skim, with approximately 60 percent of the water removed. It is then sterilised and canned. It is not that commonly used in bakeries. Once opened, store in the refrigerator.

Fresh Cream

Fresh cream is not often used as a liquid in doughs or batters, except in a few speciality products. This is mainly due to the high fat content which would act as a shortening agent rather than a moisturising agent.

Cream is more important in the production of fillings, toppings, dessert sauces, and cold desserts such as mousses and bavarois. It can also be flavoured and sweetened; however, care should be taken when doing this as an excess can cause problems like curdling and splitting during processing.

If whipping fresh cream, care should be taken; once overwhipped the only thing to do is to continue whipping it to produce butter. Whipped cream should double in volume.

Fresh cream must always be kept in the refrigerator at 0–4°C and once used in a bakery product it must be refrigerated.

Imitation Cream

New Zealanders are not familiar with imitation cream, because we have been brought up on fresh dairy cream.

Nowadays this provides an alternative to fresh cream (useful for people who cannot eat dairy products). Imitation cream is an emulsion which includes water, vegetable oils, sugar and stabilisers. Unopened imitation creams have a very long shelf life, but once opened they must be used as soon as possible.

FATS AND OILS

Fats and oils are obtained from the following sources:

- vegetables
- animals
- milks
- marine

The most common types of fats and oils are:

- butter
- cake and pastry margarine
- shortening
- lard
- high ratio shortening
- vegetable oil

Fats and oils possess the following properties in the production of bakery products:

	VOLUME	SHORTENING	LAYERING	EMULSIFYING	FRYING	FLAVOUR	EATING QUALITIES	NUTRITIONAL VALUE	KEEPING QUALITIES
Butter	•	•	•	•		•	•	•	•
Cake margarine	•	•		•			•	•	•
Pastry margarine	•	•	•				•	•	•
Shortening	•	•		•			•	•	•
Lard		•				•	•	•	•
High ratio shortening	•	•		•			•	•	•
Vegetable oil		•			•		•	•	•

Suitability of fats and oils for bakery products:

	BREAD	FERMENTED PRODUCTS	SWEET PASTRIES	SAVOURY PASTRIES	PUFF PASTRIES	POWDER AERATED PRODUCTS	CAKES	ALMOND PRODUCTS	CHOUX PASTRY
Butter		•	•		•	•	•	•	•
Cake margarine		•	•			•	•	•	•
Pastry margarine		•		•	•				
Shortening	•	•	•	•		•	•		
Lard	•	•		•					
High ratio shortening							•		
Vegetable oil	•	•				•	•		

All fats and oils should be stored in a cool place, 16–21°C, away from direct sunlight, to reduce rancidity (butter must be stored in the refrigerator before use). In some cases fats and oils must be conditioned before use (for example, for croissants the layering butter must be stored at 4°C, and when fat is required for creaming, as for cake batters, it is advisable to condition the fat to 16–21°C).

BAKING POWDER

Baking powder is a mixture of acid and alkali. The acid content is cream of tartar and the alkali content is bicarbonate of soda. They are mixed together in the ratio of two parts of cream of tartar with one part bicarbonate of soda. Preparation involves sieving the two chemicals several times to ensure even dispersal. However, it is common practice nowadays to purchase blended baking powders.

Baking powder is responsible for the aeration, final volume and often crumb structure of a product. When baking powder becomes moist during the mixing process and is heated in the oven, the reaction between the acid and alkali produces carbon dioxide. The gas lifts and pushes up the final product until the proteins from the eggs and flour have coagulated (set) during baking.

All batters and doughs containing baking powder should be kept cool (21°C or below) to prevent the gas from working on the table and not in the oven. Hence the products should not sit for too long before baking.

Baking powder should be kept in a cool, dry environment.

CREAM OF TARTAR

Cream of tartar is used in the following ways:
* added to fruit cake batters to help prevent the fruit from sinking
* sometimes added to puff pastry to mellow the flour proteins (gluten), allowing it to become more extensible

BICARBONATE OF SODA

Bicarbonate of soda is used as an aerating agent in ginger goods and also improves the colour of chocolate cake when cocoa powder is used.

NUTS

All nuts have a limited shelf life because of their high fat content. Rancidity occurs quickly if they are incorrectly stored. All nuts should be kept in a cool place, with larger quantities stored in the freezer.

The following are the most commonly used nuts.

*   Almonds: available in whole natural, blanched, split, flaked, nibbed and ground.
*   Walnuts: used either as pieces or whole for decoration.
*   Pecans: expensive and should be used in premium goods.
*   Peanuts: are the only nuts to be grown in the ground.
*   Coconut: unsweetened is the most used variety. Can be used in cakes or biscuits and is often used as a coating or decoration.
*   Hazelnuts: have a distinctive flavour and are best if roasted first.

Nuts are used extensively as an ingredient in many bakery products, including macaroons, almond pastes, frangipane filling, biscotti and walnut bread. However, it is becoming increasingly popular to use a variety of nuts for garnishing, and in the decoration of, rich deluxe fruit cakes.

FRUITS

Dried fruits include currants, sultanas, raisins, mixed peel, figs, dates, apricots, peaches, apples and bananas. All are suitable in unbaked mixtures and fillings.

Preparation may involve:

*   washing
*   drying
*   cleaning – removing stones, stalks
*   soaking (often termed as conditioning of the fruit)

The storage of most dried fruits is between four to six months in a cool dry place.

Fresh, tinned and frozen fruit give excellent visual appeal and a fresh look to many bakery products.

Fresh fruit should be used as soon as possible, but frozen and tinned fruit can be used when required.

In general, dried, fresh, tinned and frozen fruits are added towards the end of the mixing process, thus avoiding crushing and destroying the fruits' structure.

COCOA

Cocoa is the dry powder that remains after part of the cocoa butter is removed from chocolate liquor. Cocoa contains starch, which tends to absorb moisture in a cake batter; therefore, when cocoa powder is added to a batter, the amount of flour is reduced to keep the recipe balanced.

A standard rule of thumb is: for every 100 g of cocoa added to a recipe, reduce the flour by .0375 g (37.5 percent of the weight of cocoa).

CHOCOLATE COVERTURE AND CHOCOLATE COMPOUNDS

Chocolate coverture is prepared from the following ingredients: cocoa butter, cocoa and sugar which have been milled together. Chocolate coverture is expensive and is usually used when producing high class chocolate products. It also requires a process called tempering (see page 140) to ensure that the chocolate coverture sets.

Chocolate coverture is available in dark, milk and white.

Chocolate compounds are also known as chocolate coating and are prepared from the following ingredients: vegetable fats, cocoa powder, sugar, milk solids and emulsifiers. This product is much easier to use and does not require any special treatment before using. It is available in dark, milk and white chocolate compound.

White chocolate compound is very similar to chocolate compound, but the cocoa powder is replaced with milk powder.

Melting chocolate using a bain-marie (a bowl over a pot half-filled with water), gently melt the chocolate until a temperature of 37–45°C is obtained.

Caution: water or steam must not come into contact with the chocolate because it will thicken and become unusable.

To thin chocolate, use a hard vegetable fat, such as Kremelta.

SPICES

Spices are aromatic or pungent vegetable substances used to flavour food. They are obtained from various parts of different plants, including barks, buds, flowers, fruits, leaves, roots, seeds and stems.

Spices are generally whole or ground, but the latter loses its flavour rapidly, so it is important to replace spices after six months. All spices should be kept in airtight containers in a cool environment.

Spices can also be obtained in more concentrated and convenient forms, such as essential oils, extracts or essences.

Spices should be used in moderation, as too much can make the product inedible. Spices also have a retarding effect on yeast, so when using them in yeast-raised products (hot-cross buns, etc.) it is advisable to increase the yeast level.

YEAST

Yeast is a species of the fungi family of plants. The strain used by commercial bakers is called *Saccharomyces cerevisiae*. Yeast is a living single cell organism, oval in shape and can only be seen under a microscope.

Yeast is responsible for the volume in bread, buns, rolls, croissants, Danish pastries and similar products. The activity of yeast within a dough is called fermentation, which is the process by which yeast acts on sugars and changes them into carbon dioxide and alcohol. This release of gas produces the rising (often called leavening) action in yeast-raised products. The alcohol evaporates completely during, and immediately after, baking.

Yeast Requirements for Fermentation

In order for yeast to produce carbon dioxide and alcohol four conditions are required:

* time – to ferment and produce carbon dioxide
* moisture – to survive and grow

- warmth – ideal temperature is between 28–32°C
- food – food source (sugar, etc.) to feed upon and produce carbon dioxide

Without the above conditions the yeast cell will die and result in an inferior product.

Effects of Ingredients and Temperature on Yeast

- Salt slows down the activity of yeast, controlling fermentation when used at a responsible level. Excessive salt levels will retard or kill the yeast cell. You should never allow yeast to come into direct contact with salt, due to salt's hygroscopic properties (i.e., withdrawing moisture from the yeast cell).
- Sugar is a food source for yeast, but if used at too high a concentration will slow down (retard) the activity of yeast, therefore, in some cases, an increase in yeast is required to compensate (for example, for sweet doughs, Danish pastries, brioches, etc.).
- Fats used at high levels have a retarding effect upon the activity of yeast.
- Temperatures: 0°C and below – will cause some yeast cells to die
- Temperatures: 0–10°C – cause yeast activity to become slow and halted
- Temperatures: 28–32°C – yeast activity is at its optimum
- Temperatures: 32–45°C – yeast activity excessive and uncontrollable
- Temperatures: 45–55°C – yeast activity stopped and the yeast cell is destroyed

Types of Yeast

- Compressed yeast – most commonly used in commercial bakeries, can be purchased from local bakeries. Limited shelf life. Do not freeze.
- Active dried yeast – used within commercial and domestic home bakeries, can be purchased from your local supermarket (brand names: Edmonds and Elfin). Excellent shelf life unopened.
- Edmonds Surebake – a mixture of active dry yeast and bread improvers, blended specially for domestic bakeries to give soft and fine crumb structure. Excellent shelf life, refer to the use by date.

WATER

Water is obviously an essential ingredient in bread making but it has various roles in a dough.

- Water hydrates the flour proteins to produce the elastic and extensible substance called gluten which forms the dough skeleton and holds the gas produced by the yeast (often called gas retention).
- Part of the water is absorbed by the starch present in the flour.
- When the dough is mixed, some of the water is absorbed by the flour proteins and by the starch. The rest stays as free water which helps the dispersion of such ingredients as salt, sugar, etc. Yeast can only absorb food which is in a solution.
- Water plays an important part in the final finished temperature of a dough (which should be between 28–32°C for optimum yeast activity). This is controlled by the baker with experience and with a simple calculation, so the finished dough temperature should always remain consistent.
- Without the correct amount of water, the shelf life of the dough would be reduced, so it is important that the dough has the correct amount of water added. Approximately 12 percent water is evaporated during baking.

FOOD FLAVOURS

Food flavours are obtained from natural and artificial sources, for example, fruits, plants, herbs, spices and organic acids combined with alcohol and chemicals.

They are available in liquid, paste and powder form.

ASCORBIC ACID (NATURAL BREAD IMPROVER)

Ascorbic acid is an oxidising agent that stabilises the gas cell in a yeast dough and results in a baked crumb with uniform cell size. It is largely destroyed during baking. It is not common to use it in home baking.

DOUGH CONDITIONERS

Dough conditioners contain a mixture of natural and chemical substances which assist and condition the dough throughout the whole bread making process (mixing, final shaping, proofing, baking shelf life, etc.). These substances include:

- L-Cysteine
- soya flour
- emulsifiers
- specialised fats
- mould inhibitors

Dough conditioners have a beneficial effect on the following characteristics of a yeast-raised product:

- volume
- texture
- crumb and crust colour
- eating qualities
- shelf life

THE EQUIPMENT

YOUR HANDS

The most important tools are your hands. Without these you cannot feel the texture or the warmth (temperature) of your dough or batter, nor will you know the precise moment to proceed to the next delicate stage of preparing your irresistible breads, pastries and the lightest of sponges.

The more direct contact you have with your doughs or batters, the better you will get to know their idiosyncrasies.

SCALES

Scales are one of the most important pieces of equipment when weighing individual ingredients for a recipe.

Flour and other dry ingredients are difficult to weigh in measuring cups, as dry ingredients settle and compact during movement and weighing, making it difficult to get an accurate measurement or reading (a kilogram of flour, for instance, may measure 7 cups one day and $6\frac{1}{4}$ cups another day).

Several types of scales are available, but digital scales, in increments of one or two grams, are recommended for accuracy and can be purchased at most specialist kitchen stores for a reasonable price (see Sources, page 162).

THERMOMETER

Using a thermometer allows accurate temperature readings of both your ingredients and your environment. This is particularly important when dealing with yeast-related products, given that yeast is a living organism and requires a consistent temperature to produce carbon dioxide and alcohol.

A long-stemmed digital thermometer works well for reading dough and ingredient temperatures. You should also give some consideration to having an oven thermometer, because most ovens (particularly domestic ones) can be inconsistent and have a temperature variation as much as 20°C. These can be purchased from specialist kitchen stores (see Sources, page 162).

DOUGH SCRAPER OR CUTTER

This is simply a rectangular piece of stainless steel with a rolled or wooden handle and a sharp edge. The dough scraper can be used for everything from cutting or dividing the dough to scraping off excess flour that clings to your work surface and proofing cloths. A flexible plastic scraper can be used to scrape down the sides of the mixing bowl.

MIXER

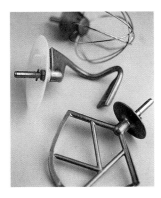

Most yeast doughs in this book can be mixed by hand or made in a domestic bread maker. If you are using a standard electric mixer, ensure that it is heavy duty and capable of generating a lot of work input (dough development/kneading). For the serious home baker, small commercial mixers can be purchased from specialist kitchen stores (see Sources, page 162).

From a commercial point of view there are many types of mixers, ranging from spiral and hi-speed mixers for yeast doughs and pastry to planetary (standard) mixers for cakes, biscuits, icing and cream fillings (the latter usually having a dough hook, paddle and whisk attachment).

DOMESTIC BREAD MAKER

There are several types of bread maker available on the New Zealand market which produce very good quality bread. However, when selecting your model, ensure that you select one with a 'mixing only' function, as this will allow you to develop your dough within the bread maker and finish it off by hand on the bench (for pizza bases, focaccia and croissants, etc.).

MIXING BOWL

It is important to have a good set of mixing bowls, ranging from 500 ml to five-litre capacity. They can be plastic, earthenware, stainless steel, glass or ceramic.

PROOFING BASKET

These are baskets made from coiled cane or plastic and are round or oval in shape (called *banneton* in France) which turn out rustic-looking loaves with a beehive pattern of flour etched on to the surface. They can be either cloth-lined or unlined naked cane and are always heavily dusted with rye flour before having the dough placed inside to proof. Once the loaf has reached its required proof size, simply turn it upside down directly on the baking stone or hearth of the oven, taking care when removing it from the proofing basket. Without a proofing basket, dough spreads too much on the tray and has trouble rising properly in the oven. A basket is better than a bowl because it allows the dough to breathe during proofing.

If you are unable to obtain specialised proofing baskets, it is simple to improvise. Buy some heavy linen (calico) from a fabric store and line or drape it over a cane or wicker basket before dusting it with rye flour. The basket should be high enough to allow the dough to double in volume.

Proofing baskets can be purchased from specialist kitchen stores (see Sources, page 162).

PROOFING CLOTH

Some breads – baguettes, rolls, braids or Vienna rolls – never see a proofing basket or even a bread tin. They are proofed instead in what the French call a *couche* (which is simply a large piece of heavy linen or canvas) that has been dusted with rye flour, then gathered around the shaped dough piece to help hold the shape of the loaves and protect the bottom and sides from drying out. Another proofing cloth is then placed on top of the dough.

Never place *couches* into a washing machine: simply scrape off the excess flour using your dough scraper and allow them to dry completely before putting away. If this is not done, the *couches* will become mouldy.

Proofing cloths can be made from heavy calico purchased from any fabric shop. Remember to overlock the edges to prevent them from fraying.

BAKING TRAYS/TINS AND MOULDS

Most breads are baked on the oven hearth or in bread tins, but there are some breads and other bakery products that require baking on trays/tins or specialised moulds (fougasse, fancy bread rolls, Danish pastries, croissants, apple strudel, biscuits, muffins, sponges, pies and tarts, etc.).

There are many different shapes and types of baking mould, including tart and quiche tins with removable bases, kugelhopf mould, panettone and pandoro moulds, baguette trays, brioche tins, fruit cake tins, hamburger trays, cake hoops and rings, tuiles trays – all of which should be kept in peak condition.

Most baking trays/tins and moulds require cleaning and greasing before each use – more usually the latter – otherwise you wash off the grease from the previous bake which can help prevent your product sticking.

Silicone and baking paper can be used instead of placing your products directly onto the baking tray, thus keeping your tray in excellent condition and ensuring your product does not stick. Silicone and baking paper can be used several times over.

An alternative is a Teflon-coated baking mat, which fits inside your baking tray and lasts for many years. All tins, trays and specialised baking moulds can be purchased from specialist kitchen stores (see Sources, page 162).

PROOFING CABINET

This is where you place your dough to rise or ferment. Within a basic proofing cabinet (known as a prover in a commercial bakery) there are two specific functions: one to supply heat (never above 40°C) and the other to supply humidity (60–80 percent relative humidity). Generally, the two functions work together.

However, in some cases more of one or less of the other is required, for example, croissants require a lower heat (28–30°C) so the butter layers do not melt, but also require a relative humidity of 60–75 percent to prevent the surface drying out.

Placing your dough in the proofing cabinet prior to baking is known as 'final proof'. In many bread recipes you are not required to place your dough in a proofing cabinet for final proofing – you simply allow the dough to rise in a warm, humid environment, often covered with a proofing cloth to prevent the dough forming a skin and drying out. This is often the case with breads from Europe.

In the domestic environment it is common practice to leave your yeasted doughs to rise or final proof in a warm draught-free place such as the hot water cupboard or even on top of your refrigerator, remembering to cover the dough lightly with a clean tea towel or a piece of plastic to prevent a crust from forming.

REFRIGERATOR

Often, bread doughs are kept in the refrigerator to slow down the action of yeast (referred to as retarding). This enables the dough to develop the flavour and texture that is often seen in European breads, especially sourdough, which require a long and cool fermentation process. At home you can place your yeasted dough in the refrigerator after it has had its first rise, then scale and final mould it many hours later (in much the same way as brioche is made).

FREEZER

Can be used for storage of unbaked and baked products. In general, the faster you freeze, the better your product will be once it has been through its freeze-thaw cycle.

FINE MESH SIEVE

A fine mesh sieve is used to sift or dust rye flour over your proofing cloths and baskets. You may also dust rye flour over your dough prior to baking so that you can slash the dough and give it your artistic signature.

When dusting with icing sugar, tap the sieve lightly to ensure even dusting.

Larger sieves can be used for incorporating several dry ingredients together before being combined into a cake batter.

RAZOR BLADE OR DOUGH SLASHING KNIFE

The artistic signature of each baker is slashed or cut into the loaf just before the loaf is placed in the oven (at 75 percent of final proof to avoid the dough piece collapsing). This artistic signature is simply done with a double-edged razor blade threaded onto a piece of steel or bamboo skewer or a special small serrated knife. To give an attractive appearance, each loaf is cut so that it has a planned and predictable place at which to burst and achieve the oven spring it needs to develop to its full potential. The cut is as important as any other process in bread making. It must be done at the correct time and at the correct angle to prevent the dough from collapsing before being placed into the oven. Practice makes perfect!

SCISSORS

If you are baking rolls, instead of slashing them you can snip the tops with scissors and create peaks that toast nicely in the oven, giving a little extra crunch when eating. However, this must be done at 75 percent of final proof to avoid the dough piece collapsing.

BAKER'S PEEL

Baker's peels are used at the critical moment in the baking process when you transfer the dough from its proofing place to the oven. At this stage, if you are not careful you can deflate the dough, preventing it from acquiring its correct shape. If using a baker's peel to transfer your dough piece, lightly dust your peel's head with semolina flour and gently place or roll your dough piece onto it. Open your oven door and with a quick forward and backwards jerk, slide your dough piece on to the oven's hearth or baking stone. Again, practice makes perfect!

Commercial bakeries also use baker's peels for loading and unloading the oven filled with trays of cakes, biscuits and pastries. Peels are usually made from wood and have very long handles, enabling the baker to reach to the back of the oven. When using a domestic oven, use a thin wooden board (in the shape of a peel, with a short handle) that has been sharpened at the end.

Peels can be purchased at most specialist kitchen stores for a reasonable price (see Sources, page 162).

BAKING STONE

It is best to bake bread on the oven hearth or on baking stones. They provide insulated and solid heat, which helps the bread bake more evenly than it would on a metal baking tray. The hearth or oven stones absorb the moisture from the dough as it bakes, which gives the loaf a crispier bottom and chewier crust.

For a domestic oven, baking stones can be purchased from specialist kitchen stores (see Sources, page 162) or you could even get your local ceramic tile specialist to cut one to suit your oven tray size. When you first receive your baking stone, condition it in the oven at a low temperature for several hours or overnight so it will not crack when you turn the heat up high to bake your bread.

SPRAY BOTTLE OR PLANT MISTER

Within the first few minutes of baking bread, you want to create a moist, hot environment. Most commercial bakeries have steam-injected ovens, but to simulate this in your domestic oven, spray hot water directly onto the sides and hearth or baking stone just before placing your dough piece in. Lightly spray the inside of the oven two or three times within the first five minutes of baking. Ensure that you use hot water because spraying with cold water will lower the oven temperature too drastically. Another way to create steam is to place a tray full of water in the bottom of your oven.

A spray bottle can also be useful when applying seeds, cheese, etc., to your dough piece prior to baking. Simply spray the dough piece and apply seeds or cheese, etc.

If you notice that during the final proofing stage your dough piece is skinning and crusting over, you must ensure that the crusting is removed as quickly as possible because it prevents the dough from rising and achieving its correct volume. Lightly spray the surface with warm water.

OVEN

There is no need for the home baker to invest thousands of dollars in a 'state of the art' commercial oven – just make a few adjustments to your domestic oven. Spray your oven with hot water or place a tray full of water in the oven to create a steamy, humid atmosphere, and place a baking stone at the bottom of your oven to simulate a traditional friendly bread-baking oven. The same oven will produce excellent pastry and cake products.

Before placing your products into the oven always check that the oven is:

- set at the correct temperature for the product
- is up to that correct temperature (usually assessed by checking whether the thermostat light has switched off)

COOLING RACK

Always place your baked loaf directly onto a cooling rack. This enables air circulation around the whole loaf and prevents the bottom from sweating and going soggy.

When cooling cake-related products, it is better to leave the cake in the tin for 5–10 minutes to allow the cake to settle before turning out onto a cooling rack or wire to cool.

SERRATED KNIFE

When cutting any bakery product use the correct knife. For baked bread and cakes use a sharp, serrated knife; use dry when cutting bread, and dip in hot water when cutting cakes such as gateaux and torten to ensure a clean and crumb-free cut.

ROLLING PIN AND PASTRY SHEETER

Very few breads require the use of a rolling pin for final shaping. The exceptions are croissants, Danish pastries, hamburgers, focaccia, panini and chelsea buns. Therefore, the rolling pin or pastry sheeter is best suited to pastry products.

Select either the French variety of rolling pin, which is a thin solid cylinder of wood, or the thicker American/English kind, which has handles that are mounted on ball bearings. Whichever you choose, make sure it is at least 35–40 cm in length.

Pastry sheeters are found in almost every commercial bakery, usually having one canvas conveyor belt either side of two automatic revolving rollers set on top of each other. The rollers can be opened and closed to reduce the thickness of the pastry.

PASTRY DOCKER

A spiked mini rolling pin set on a handle is the best way to describe this piece of baking equipment. It is used to dock or puncture puff pastry to stop it from rising, allowing the steam to escape during baking (often called docking).

A pastry docker can also be used to dock the top of dough pieces to give a decorative effect.

PASTRY BRUSH

The ever versatile pastry brush has many uses, for instance, brushing olive oil on focaccia and panini after baking, dusting flour off the surface of dough or pastry, glazing the tops of pies, tarts, pastries, biscuits and even bread with egg wash, washing interior edges of pastry turnovers or calzone with water so they stick together during baking, and cleaning the sides of a copper pot during the boiling of sugar for sugar decorating.

PASTRY BAG AND PIPING TUBE

Pastry bags (also called savoys or piping bags) and piping tubes (also called piping nozzles) are used for making borders, inscriptions, designs, flowers and many other decorations out of icing and cream fillings. The basic tubes are as follows: plain, star, rose, leaf, and ribbon or basket-weave. Many other specialised tubes are available for unusual shapes, however, the plain and star tubes are by far the most important.

The easiest way to use a pastry bag and piping tube is to fit the tube inside the pastry bag, then push the bag into the tube to prevent the icing from flowing straight out during filling. Turn back the top of the bag and then fill the bag no more than two-thirds full. Gather the top of the bag with one hand and twist it securely. Place the other hand just above the tube and apply even pressure at the top of the bag so that the filling flows smoothly and evenly from the tube.

PASTRY/BISCUIT CUTTER

There are many different shapes and sizes of pastry or biscuit cutter, ranging from plain, crinkled, round, square and oblong, to gingerbread people and teddy bears, etc. Generally, the round cutters are the most popular and are used for cutting discs of pastry so they can line pastry cases, tart and flan rings. After washing your cutters, dry them well to prevent any rusting or metal deterioration, then store in a container to protect them from damage.

PASTRY WHEEL

Imagine 8–10 pizza cutters (the wheel type) joined together on an adjustable concertina-type brace which can be enlarged or retracted. Pastry wheels are used when you require many items of the same shape to be cut from one large sheet of pastry (usually square, rectangle, triangle or diamond) or when you require the top of your cakes or slices to be marked to achieve a consistent yield time after time.

PALETTE KNIFE

The palette knife is to a baker what a trowel is to a brick layer. These are thin, flexible, round-ended, blunt-edged knives that are used for spreading creams, jams, icing and royal icing, etc., onto slices, sponges, cakes and gateaux.

Palette knives come in various sizes and are either straight or trowel-shaped (the latter is often referred to as a crank-handled palette knife).

MEASURING CUPS AND SPOONS

Some measurements given in this book are given in spoons and cups as well as metric measurements. (In any case, we recommend that all ingredients are weighed on a set of accurate scales.) If you decide to measure your ingredients with spoons and cups ensure that you have purchased your measuring implements from a specialist kitchen shop. The standard domestic teaspoon, tablespoon and cup will vary from kitchen to kitchen and even country to country, and if used will result in an inferior finished baked product.

FORMULAS AND MEASUREMENTS

SCALING INGREDIENTS

All ingredients must be measured accurately. Water, liquid milk and beaten eggs (commonly called egg pulp) may be measured by volume. They are scaled at one kilogram per litre i.e., 1.000 kg of water = 1.000 litre of water. However, if quantities are large, it is advisable to weigh these ingredients on an accurate set of scales.

RECIPE BALANCE

Recipes are balanced formulations, therefore if you add too much of one ingredient this will, in turn, upset another ingredient and unbalance the recipe. Special care must be taken when measuring salt, baking powder, spices, sugar and other ingredients used in small amounts, as it is often the case that the smaller the amount the more effect it has on the finished baked product.

BAKER'S PERCENTAGES

Bakers use a simple but versatile system of percentages for expressing their formulas or recipes. Baker's percentages indicate the quantities of each item that would be required if 100 kg of flour were used. In other words, each ingredient is expressed as a percentage of the total flour weight. To put it differently, the percentage of each ingredient is its total weight divided by the weight of the flour, multiplied by 100. For example:

$$\frac{\text{Total weight of ingredient}}{\text{Total weight of flour}} \times 100 = \% \text{ of ingredient}$$

The flour is always expressed as 100 percent. If two kinds of flour are used, their total is still 100 percent. Any ingredient that weighs the same as the flour is also expressed as 100 percent. See the formulations below to understand how these percentages are used. Check the figures with the above equation to make sure you understand them.

WHITE BREAD FORMULATION

INGREDIENT	WEIGHT	%
Bread flour	5.000 kg	100
Salt	.100 kg	2
Sugar	.050 kg	1
Fat	.150 kg	3
Yeast	.150 kg	3
Water	2.800 lt	56
Total weight	8.250 kg	
Yield @ .550 kg	15	

CAKE FORMULATION

INGREDIENT	WEIGHT	%
Ingredient	Weight	%
Cake flour	2.500 kg	100
Sugar	2.500 kg	100
Baking powder	.125 kg	5
Salt	.063 kg	2.5
Shortening	1.250 kg	50
Milk	1.500 lt	60
Egg whites	1.500 lt	60
Total weight	9.438 kg	
Yield @ .500 kg	18.8	

Advantages of using baker's percentages The formulations or recipes are easy to adapt for any yield, and single ingredients may be varied and other ingredients added without changing the whole formulation. For example, you can add blueberries to your muffin formulation and the percentages of all the other ingredients will stay the same.

METRIC CONVERSIONS

All recipes in this book are in the metric system. This system has one basic unit for each type of measurement:

- the gram and kilogram are the basic units of weight
- the litre is the basic unit for volume
- the centimetre and metre are the basic units of length
- the degree celsius is the basic unit of temperature

To convert Celsius (C) to Fahrenheit (F):
Formula: F – 32 ÷ 9 x 5 = C
Example: 425°F (– 32 ÷ 9 x 5) = 218°C

To convert Fahrenheit (F) to Celsius (C):
Formula: C ÷ 5 x 9 + 32 = F
Example: 218°C (÷ 5 x 9 + 32) = 424°F

To convert ounces (oz) to grams (g):
Conversion: 1 ounce = 28.4 grams
Example: 16 oz x 28.4 g = 454.4 grams

To convert pounds (lb) to kilograms (kg):
Conversion: 1 lb = .454 grams (1 lb = 16oz)
Example: 1 lb 3 oz = 19 oz x 28.4 g = .539 kilograms

Calculating the required water temperature to achieve a finished dough temperature It is important when working with yeast doughs that you understand that for the yeast to produce carbon dioxide it must have favourable conditions to work in. One of the most important conditions is temperature (refer to Yeast in the Ingredients section).

All yeast-raised recipes have a finished dough temperature figure. This tells you the best temperature for the yeast to operate in once the dough has completed mixing. The following calculation best explains the method that should be used with all yeast-raised recipes in this book (Note: this is the calculation used for mixing yeast-raised doughs by hand).

- Required finished dough temperature x 2
- Subtract the flour temperature
- Add adjustment for hand mixing
- Equals required water temperature

Example:	**Finished dough temperature**	**29°C**
	Finished dough temperature x 2 =	58°C
	Subtract flour temperature (20°C)	−20°C
		38°C
	Add adjustment for hand mixing	+ 3°C
	Equals required water temperature	**41°C**

In the domestic environment, when mixing your dough by hand, a general rule of thumb for the required water temperature is:

- body or blood temperature (approximately 37°C)

ALL ABOUT BREAD

BASIC INGREDIENTS

There are four main ingredients required to make successful bread:

- strong, good quality bread flour
- salt
- yeast (commercial or natural)
- water

All other ingredients used to make bread are often called enriching agents or bread improvers, for example, sugar, fats or oils, eggs, milk, dried fruits, etc.

Basic ingredient functions

Strong flour is the most important ingredient in bread. Without the protein (gluten) present in the flour there could not be bread as we know it; therefore, the protein content must be of excellent quality and quantity. During the baking process the starch gelatinises and protein coagulates to provide the structure and framework of the baked loaf or roll. Of course, this goes hand in hand with correct mixing or kneading, which is explained in further detail later in this section.

Salt provides flavour to bread, along with strengthening the gluten. Used at its recommended usage rate, salt controls the fermentation of yeast. If used in excessive amounts, salt retards or kills the yeast cells.

Yeast is used as the aerating agent in bread doughs. Without yeast the loaf or roll would be small in volume and very dense in texture.

The main functions of yeast in the production of bread are:

- production of carbon dioxide for aeration
- development of the gluten network through the action of fermentation
- development of the bread flavour and aroma

Water levels provide the dough consistency; however, this level can be quite variable depending on the quality of flour and other ingredients used. Adjustments may be necessary to produce good quality bread. The water also controls the dough temperature which has an influence on the speed of fermentation, that is, the colder the water, the colder the dough, the slower the yeast produces carbon dioxide.

BREAD MAKING PROCESSES

There are four commonly used bread making processes:

Bulk fermentation is used to achieve full-flavoured bread. It requires no special ingredient consideration but needs time to produce from start to finished baked loaf. This process is the most commonly used in the domestic environment.

No-time is for breads requiring only a short time from the raw ingredient stage to the finished baked loaf (often only one-and-a-half hours). Commonly used in supermarket in-store bakeries and many hot bread shops. This process requires special oxidising ingredients and dough conditioners such as ascorbic acid, emulsifiers, enzymes, L-Cysteine, etc. This process is not commonly used in the domestic environment.

Sponge and dough is the oldest method of making bread, often using a starter dough which may contain either commercial baker's yeast or wild natural yeasts. Bread produced using this method has a wonderful texture, flavour and aroma, for example, traditional sourdough and many other European breads. Producing bread using this method requires experience, knowledge, passion, understanding and plenty of tender loving care. This process is commonly used in the domestic environment.

Mechanical dough development (MDD) was developed in the 1970s for the large commercial plant bakeries that required a fast mixing and processing bread to maximise their production. This process is largely the same as the no-time process with a shorter mixing time operated under vacuum to achieve a fine cell structure that is required for sliced sandwich breads, etc. This process is not commonly used in the domestic environment.

STEPS IN YEAST-RAISED PRODUCTION
There are 12 basic steps that are used in the production of yeast-raised products. These steps are generally applied to all yeast products, with some variations depending on the required finished product.

STEPS	BULK FERMENTATION	NO-TIME	SPONGE & DOUGH	MECHANICAL DOUGH DEVELOPMENT
Scaling ingredients	•	•	•	•
Preparation of sponge or starter			•	
Mixing or kneading	•	•	•	•
Bulk fermentation	•		•	
Knocking back	•		•	
Dividing or scaling	•	•	•	•
Rounding	•	•	•	•
Intermediate proof	•	•	•	•
Final make up & placing on trays	•	•	•	•
Final proof	•	•	•	•
Cutting, seeding, dusting, etc.	•	•	•	•
Baking	•	•	•	•
Cooling	•	•	•	•
Storing	•	•	•	•

Scaling ingredients Special care must be taken when measuring salt, sugar and spices, as these ingredients will have an effect on the fermentation process.

Preparation of a sponge or starter Some yeast-raised doughs require a sponge or starter dough. This step requires forward planning and consists of a two-stage process. A sponge is a basic dough made from the four main ingredients: flour, salt, yeast and water. The sponge is then allowed to ferment for 18 hours in bulk or in some cases until the sponge falls back onto itself. The speed of fermentation can be controlled by the levels of salt and yeast and also by the temperature of the water used.

A starter dough is commonly used in the production of sourdough-type breads that require a crisp crust, irregular crumb and a wonderful tarty fermented flavour and aroma. The starter can take 14 days to raise from scratch: nine to grow the culture and five to build the starter to the strength you require to bake a loaf of bread. The starter culture consists of only flour and water, which attract wild natural yeasts and bacteria.

Don't be put off by the length of time it takes to grow the starter, as you only have to grow it once. After that, as long as you feed and maintain it, your starter will be ready to use over and over again. See the recipe and instructions in this section for preparing a sourdough starter, or leaven as it is commonly known in France.

Mixing or kneading This is one of the most important steps and should not be taken for granted, especially when kneading your dough by hand, as one of the most common faults in bread is under mixing, resulting in a poor volume loaf. There are two purposes of mixing:

(i)   combining the ingredients into a dough, hydrating the gluten and distributing the yeast are accomplished during the first stage of mixing

(ii)   the remaining time is required for developing the gluten network and allowing air and gases to be trapped within the dough (see Understanding Dough Development, page 38)

All mixing times that relate to yeast-raised products are guidelines only. You must learn by feel and sight when your dough has been fully developed. A correctly developed dough should be smooth, elastic and silky.

IMPORTANCE OF DOUGH TEMPERATURE

During any type of mixing, whether in a mixer or by hand, the dough will increase in temperature, caused by friction. It is important that you achieve the correct finished dough temperature so that your dough is not going to ferment too fast or in some cases too slowly, resulting in poor quality baked products (see the Formulas and Measurements section, page 30, on how to calculate the required water temperature to achieve the desired finished dough temperature).

Achieving the correct finished dough temperature lets you know what your dough is doing and how it will react within the conditions and environment, for example, during winter or summer. You should always take and record your dough temperature once you have developed your dough.

Most doughs within this book require a finished dough temperature between 27–32°C unless specified in the recipe.

STEPS IN MIXING AND KNEADING BY HAND

Mixing or kneading should be fun and enjoyable. Ensure that you knead on a solid surface with plenty of space and that the bench is of a suitable height.

The first four steps can be done in a large bowl if you prefer.

Make a well with the flour in the middle of the bench. Sprinkle the other dry ingredients around the edge.

Slowly add the water, taking care not to overflow the well. Keep a small amount of water back to adjust the dough to the correct consistency. The yeast or starter must be added at this stage.

Using your fingertips, slowly mix in a circular motion, picking up the dry ingredients from around the outside. Be careful not to break the well and cause the liquids to flow out.

At this stage, you should have a porridge-like consistency. Continue to mix but now gather the flour from the outside, using your scraper, to form a firm dough. Keep one hand clean at this stage.

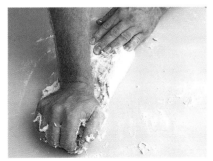

Clean the bench and your hands with your scraper. At this stage, begin to knead your dough by the traditional method of turning, folding and pushing with the heel of your hand repeatedly. Adjust your dough consistency by adding water or liquid at this early stage of kneading.

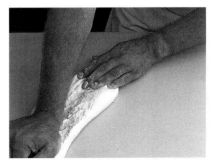

Continue to knead the dough using the method described. This should take anywhere from 10–15 minutes, and your dough should become smooth, silky and elastic. See Understanding Dough Development below.

UNDERSTANDING DOUGH DEVELOPMENT

This is one of the most important steps in successful bread making. Good bread flour contains a protein called gluten which gives structure and strength to all yeast-raised goods.

In order for gluten to be developed, the proteins (glutenin and gliadin) must first absorb water or liquids, then, as the dough is mixed or kneaded, the gluten forms long, elastic and rubbery strands, known as the gluten network.

As the dough begins to rise the gluten network captures the gases (produced by the yeast) in tiny pockets or cells and allows the dough to rise and expand. If the gluten network within the dough has not been correctly developed, these gases will escape, resulting in a collapsed small volume loaf.

There are many factors that determine when a dough is developed:

- temperature of water
- speed of mixing or kneading
- selection and amounts of raw ingredients; high fat and sugar doughs take less time to develop due to the 'shortening' effect these ingredients have on the gluten network

The dough is developed when:

(i) the dough clears from the sides of the mixing bowl, assuming that the correct liquid amounts have been used

(ii) the dough has a smooth, silky and elastic texture

(iii) a small piece of dough can be stretched to achieve a smooth satiny sheen which is elastic and extensible (often called the 'stretch test' – see below)

An under-developed dough. Notice the rough and easily broken texture of the dough when stretched out.

A correctly developed dough: smooth, elastic and extensible when stretched.

Bulk fermentation, or first rising as it is sometimes called. This term is used to describe the length of time that the dough is allowed to ferment in bulk. The bulk fermentation period is measured from the end of mixing to the beginning of scaling or dividing the dough. This period can be from 1–18 hours depending on the levels of salt and yeast in the recipe, as well as the dough temperature, which should be between 25–27°C.

During bulk fermentation the following conditions must be observed:

(i) place the dough into a lightly oiled container large enough to allow the dough to double in size

(ii)   the dough must be covered to prevent the dough surface from skinning

(iii) place the dough in an environment where the temperature will remain constant (for example, the hot water cupboard)

Knocking back During the bulk fermentation period the dough increases in volume (often double), due to the gases given off by the yeast. To prevent the gases from escaping prematurely the dough is gently 'knocked back' or 'punched down', generally three-quarters of the way through the bulk fermentation period. This is done by hand, by gently pushing, punching and folding the dough. Knocking back is done for the following reasons:

- to expel the gases and revitalise the yeast's activity
- to even out the dough temperature because the outside of the dough will be colder than the inside
- to stimulate and help develop the gluten network
- to even out the cell structure

Once the knocking back stage has been completed, the dough is returned to the container and covered until it is required for scaling. Bulk fermentation and knocking back times are included in the relevant recipes within this book.

Dividing or scaling This takes place directly when the dough has either completed its mixing or bulk fermentation period. Using your scales and dough scraper, gently divide your dough into the required sizes and weights. This should be done as quickly as possible to avoid excessive fermentation.

Rounding After scaling, the dough pieces are shaped into smooth, round balls. This assists the gases within the fermenting dough to remain. Another important reason why this stage is included is to pre-shape the dough before it undergoes its final shaping. To achieve this, cup your hand or hands over the dough piece, and with a little pressure begin to move your dough in a circular motion making sure that the dough is in contact with the bench all the time. Avoid rounding on a floured surface, as you want the dough to grip the bench. This movement stretches the surface of the dough so that it is completely smooth except for a seam at the bottom where the dough has gripped the bench (see photograph to the right).

Intermediate proof This is sometimes referred to as 'first proof', 'recovery time' or 'bench time'. This is a resting period of 10–15 minutes that takes place between rounding and final make up or shaping, allowing the gluten network to relax. If insufficient intermediate proof time is given, the dough piece will tear and become misshapen during final make up or shaping. During the intermediate proof you must cover your dough piece with a sheet of plastic, dough cloth, or a clean tea towel to stop the dough surface from skinning.

Final make up and placing on trays Once the dough piece has had its intermediate proof, mould it into its final shape before placing into bread tins, proofing baskets or onto baking trays. Correct make up or moulding is critical to the finished baked loaf or roll. All moulded bread doughs have a seam and the seam should always be placed bottom side down (with the exception of cane proofing baskets where the smooth surface should be placed at the bottom). This avoids splitting during the baking process.

Once the final shaping has taken place, toppings can be put onto the dough piece before it enters the final proof stage, for example, sesame and poppy seeds, cheese, flour, etc.

There are many great, effective shapes that breads, rolls and buns can take. These techniques will be explained and shown in the recipe section of this book.

Final proof Often known as 'proofing'. This is critical for product quality and should be monitored closely. Once the dough is ready to enter the prover there are three main areas that require attention:

(i) temperature – proofing temperatures should be higher than the dough temperature, as this prevents the dough from chilling and allows the yeast to function effectively. The ideal temperature should be 35–40°C.

(ii) humidity – moisture in the air. The requirement for humidity in final proofing is to prevent drying of the dough piece. Skinning prevents a glossy crust forming during steaming and baking. Lack of humidity will slow proofing. Higher humidity will result in undesirably fast proofing and an inferior product. In the domestic environment a spray bottle can be used to prevent skinning during proofing.

(iii) time – proof times depend upon dough size, final dough temperature, yeast levels and even ingredients used; 45–90 minutes are common proof times.

If a prover is not available, come as close to the above conditions as possible by covering the products loosely to retain the moisture and setting them in a warm place (hot water cupboard or similar).

How do we determine when a dough piece is under- or over-proofed or proofed to its correct size when using the indentation test?

Under-proofed This is when you lightly press your finger into the side of the dough and the indentation 'springs' out quickly to its original shape. More proof time is required.
Correct proof When you lightly press your finger into the side of the dough, the indentation slowly springs back, but does not obtain its original shape. It leaves a small indentation mark. At this stage, the dough piece is ready to enter the oven.
Over-proofed When lightly pressed, the dough piece will collapse and the indentation mark will not spring back. Place the dough piece into the oven as soon as possible at the correct oven temperature. The product, however, will be of poor quality.

Cutting, seeding and dusting This is done for the decorative appearance of the finished baked loaf or roll.

* Cutting or slashing: see the Equipment section under Razor Blade or Slashing Knife for detailed information.

* Seeding is done either after the final shape or just before the fully proofed loaf or rolls enter the oven. If the latter is done then the loaf or rolls need to be lightly sprayed with water before the seeds are sprinkled on. Grated cheese can also be applied at this stage.

* Dusting the loaf or rolls with flour at full proof allows the flour to bake onto the product. Dusting and cutting are normally done hand in hand with each other to achieve a decorative pattern.

Cutting or slashing a boule – notice the angle of the blade.

Baking Proofed doughs are fragile until the flour proteins have been coagulated (set) by baking. The dough should be handled with care when being loaded into the preheated oven. The heat causes the yeast, in the last stages of life, to lift the dough one more time before it is killed by the excessive heat; this is called 'oven spring'. For this to happen the oven must be hot and moist. Professional bakers use steam-injected ovens which prevent the crust from drying out and being dull in colour. (The gelatinisation that occurs between the steam in the oven and the starch in the dough gives the loaf or roll its characteristic 'bloom'.) In the domestic oven, spray the sides and baking stone of the oven with warm water one minute before putting the dough piece into the oven. Repeat this two to three times within the first five minutes of baking. Ensure that you only open the door narrowly to avoid excessive steam and heat loss each time you spray. Once your dough piece is in the oven, avoid spraying it directly with the water, as this will cause an inferior finished product.

Baking on baking stones or the hearth of the oven To load the oven, place the proofed dough piece or pieces onto peels that have been well-dusted with semolina or cornmeal. Slide the peel into the oven; then, with a quick forward and backward jerk, slide the dough piece onto the baking stone or hearth of the oven.

Baking on trays or in tins Many products, such as rolls, buns and tin breads, are baked on trays or in tins which are directly placed onto the baking stones or the hearth of the oven. However, these are not known as traditional hearth breads.

Baking the ideal product is dependent on time, temperature and dough weight.
*   Large dough pieces (400–500 g) require high temperatures and longer baking periods, i.e., 220–230°C for 30–40 minutes.
*   Small dough pieces (100–200 g) require significantly less time and lower baking temperatures, i.e., 200–210°C for 12–18 minutes.

BAKING GUIDELINES

The longer the baking time:
*   the thicker the crust
*   the greater the moisture loss
*   the darker the crust colour

The higher the baking temperature:
*   the shorter the baking time
*   the thinner the product crust
*   the more risk the larger dough pieces will be underbaked and may collapse

The lower the baking temperature:
*   the longer the total baking time
*   the thicker the product crust
*   the more oven spring

To tell if a loaf of bread is correctly baked, tap the bottom, and if it sounds hollow, the loaf is correctly baked.

Cooling The flavour and aroma do not fully develop until the loaf has cooled completely. Always place your baked breads directly onto a cooling rack or wire to prevent sweating.

Storing Breads to be served within eight hours may be left in the open air or in a paper bag. Breads that are to retain a crust must not be packaged, as this will cause the crust to soften and become leathery. If storing your bread in the freezer, place it into a plastic bag to extend its shelf life. Never place bread into the refrigerator as this speeds up the staling process.

FAULTS IN BREAD & YEAST-RAISED PRODUCTS

FAULTS / CAUSES	Overmature dough	Tight dough	Slack dough	Underproof	Overproof	Baking time too long	Baking temp too low	Baking temp too high	Insufficient steam in oven	Flour used too weak	Poor final moulding	Lack of salt	Dough temp too high	Undermising of dough	Excessive steam in prover	Excessive steam in oven	Excessive salt	Insufficient yeast	Excessive sugar
Poor volume & oven spring		•		•	•		•	•		•		•		•	•			•	
Flat appearance	•		•		•		•			•		•		•		•	•		
Pale crust colour	•						•					•				•		•	
Excessive crust colour								•	•								•		•
Thick crust		•				•	•	•						•					
Unstable internal open crumb	•	•			•					•	•		•				•		•
Poor crumb colour	•		•	•	•					•	•		•				•		
Poor shape	•	•	•	•	•			•			•								
Wrinkled crust					•											•			
Poor shelf life	•	•		•	•	•				•		•							

ALL ABOUT CAKES, SPONGES & BISCUITS

BASIC INGREDIENTS

Cakes There are four main ingredients that are required to make successful cakes:

* soft flour
* fresh eggs
* sugar
* butter

A cake baked with equal parts of each of the above ingredients is often referred to as a pound cake:

> 1 lb soft flour
>
> 1 lb fresh eggs
>
> 1 lb sugar
>
> 1 lb butter

The pound has now been replaced with grams and kilograms, but the principle remains the same.

Many other ingredients are added to further enrich the cake and aid its keeping qualities, for example, liquid milk, water, special emulsifiers, dried fruit, chocolate and flavours, baking powders, etc.

Sponges The basic ingredients required to make a light textured sponge are:

* soft flour
* sugar
* fresh eggs

Again, many other ingredients can be added to increase its keeping qualities and also add texture and flavour, for example, melted butter, special emulsifiers, water, baking powders, etc.

Biscuits The basic ingredients required to make biscuits vary depending on size, texture, flavour, etc. However, the following can be used as a base, with many other ingredients being added to obtain a desired texture, flavour or eye appeal, for example, chocolate chips, peanuts, cocoa, baking powder, dried fruit, etc.

* soft flour
* sugar
* butter
* fresh eggs

BASIC INGREDIENT FUNCTIONS

Flour and eggs These two ingredients alone have the ability to form a structure which will expand during baking and coagulate (set) when a high enough temperature has been reached. Remember that both contain protein, flour (gluten) and eggs (albumin).

Eggs contain a natural emulsifier called lecithin, which assists in combining two substances or ingredients which do not normally go together: fats and water. This is known as an emulsion.

Butter or fats are added to cake batters to assist in aeration, to supply flavour and to make the cakes more tender to eat. They also play an important part in shortening the flour proteins, which allow the cake to expand during the baking process. Fats also assist in the keeping quality of the cake.

Sugar is used to produce tenderness, sweetness and crust colour. Sugar also assists in aeration and can be regarded as an 'opening agent', opening the structure of the cake which increases the volume in the finished baked product. This is only true if the butter and sugar are beaten until light and fluffy.

Milk is sometimes substituted for egg in a recipe and acts as a moistening agent. Milk, or any liquid, is generally regarded as a 'closing agent', closing the structure of the cake which reduces the volume in the finished baked product.

Baking powder is used to aerate the cake during the baking process by producing carbon dioxide in the presence of moisture and heat. Baking powder is regarded as an 'opening agent'. Too little baking powder will result in a dense, poor volume cake, while excessive baking powder will result in an open texture with a darkened crumb, and often the cake will sink in the middle.

MIXING METHODS

In order for cakes and sponges to be light and airy in texture this requires beating or whipping air into the batter. This is known as aeration. Aeration can be achieved through many different methods for cakes, sponges and biscuits. Let's take a closer look at the mixing methods required for each.

All cake and sponge batters should have a final batter temperature of 18–24°C; therefore, it may be necessary to warm the eggs and other liquids to room temperature (21°C) before adding to the batter.

Cakes

Sugar Batter or Creaming Method
1. Cream together the sugar and softened fat until light, creamy and fluffy.
2. Add warmed eggs in 4–5 additions. Incorporate each addition thoroughly.
3. Sieve together the dry ingredients, add to the above and mix until a smooth clear batter is obtained. Do not overmix as this will result in a tough cake with small volume.

Note: if milk or other liquids are to be incorporated, this should be done when the batter is half mixed, thus avoiding overmixing.

Flour Batter or Blending Method
1. Mix the sugar with the warmed eggs and whisk until a thick spongelike consistency is achieved, commonly know as the ribbon stage (see photograph).
2. Cream the fat with an equal amount of flour.
3. Add (1) to (2) in four additions, blending each addition of sponge in well to the fat/flour mixture.

Eggs and sugar that have been whipped to the ribbon stage. Ribbon stage is when a mixture can hold its own weight for 10 seconds or more. Notice the thick sponge-like consistency.

4. Blend in the remainder of the flour, so that a smooth lump-free mixture is formed.
5. Lastly, add any other ingredients, such as milk, dried fruits, etc., blending in carefully to ensure even distribution.

Sponges

Traditional Method
1. Whisk together the warmed eggs and sugar to the ribbon stage (see photograph on opposite page).
2. Sieve the flour and carefully fold through the sponge. Avoid overmixing.
3. Once deposited into tins you must bake immediately.

Emulsified or All-in Method
1. Mix together the egg, water and sponge emulsifier.
2. Sieve together the dry ingredients, add to the above and blend to form a pastelike consistency.
3. Whisk on top speed for 5 minutes or until a thick sponge is reached (ribbon stage).
4. Once deposited in the tin this sponge can stand for 30–60 minutes before entering the oven.

Note: this method is used in commercial bakeries due to the special sponge emulsifiers which produce an excellent quality sponge.

Biscuits

Creaming Method
1. Beat together the sugar and softened fat until light and creamy.
2. Add the egg in 4–5 additions, beating well during each addition.
3. Sieve the dry ingredients and blend in on low speed until the batter is smooth and clear.

Note: this method is best suited to piped biscuits, for example, Viennese, Melting Moments, Toffee Biscuits, etc.

Blending Method
1. Blend together the sugar and softened fat until the two are well combined and soft. Do not cream or aerate this mixture.
2. Add the eggs all at once (if required) and slowly blend in. Do not cream or aerate the mixture at this stage.
3. Sieve the dry ingredients and blend in until the dough has cleared the sides of the mixing bowl and formed a solid mass.

Note: this method is best suited to rolled, refrigerated, cut and pressed biscuits, for example, Speculaas, Shortbread, Chocolate Chip, etc.

Viennese biscuits being piped onto a baking tray.

POINTS TO CONSIDER WHEN PROCESSING CAKES AND SPONGES

Cakes

1. Prepare all ingredients correctly and measure your ingredients accurately.
2. Always adhere to the procedures and mixing times stated in the recipe.
3. Scrape down the sides of the bowl frequently to ensure an even mixture is achieved.
4. Once the flour has been added avoid overmixing the batter.
5. Always check that the oven is preheated and set on the correct baking temperature required for the product.
6. Place the cakes into the oven as soon as possible to avoid the loss of aeration.

Sponges

1. Always ensure that your equipment is free from grease.
2. Prepare all ingredients correctly and measure your ingredients accurately.
3. Always adhere to the procedures and mixing times stated in the recipe.
4. If using the traditional method, avoid overmixing when folding in the flour, as this will result in a loss of volume in the finished baked product. Bake immediately.
5. Always check that the oven is preheated and set on the correct baking temperature required for the product.

WHAT HAPPENS DURING THE BAKING PROCESS?

When a cake or sponge batter goes into the oven many things happen:

1. The fat melts, causing the batter to flow level.
2. As the temperature rises, the batter becomes quite fluid and if knocked at this stage the cake could lose volume.
3. The air trapped during the creaming stage begins to expand and, as carbon dioxide is given off by the baking powder (if used), the bubbles become larger and join together.
4. The volume of the batter increases and the proteins of the flour and egg stretch to accommodate the expanding gases.
5. Steam is also produced as boiling point is reached, which assists in aeration.
6. As the heat increases, the starch of the flour begins to gelatinise and takes up much of the moisture present.
7. The expanding proteins begin to coagulate (set).
8. The centre of the cake is the last to be baked.
9. The sugar near the crust caramelises to give a golden brown colour.
10. The cake is baked when it springs back after being lightly pressed with your fingertips.

BAKING GUIDELINES

This is a general guide to the baking of cakes and sponges. All times and temperatures are guides only and will vary from oven to oven.

PRODUCT	TEMPERATURE	TIME (VARIABLE)
Fruit Cakes	160–170°C	2–4 hours
Madeira-style Cakes	170–180°C	20–30 minutes
Muffins	180–190°C	15–18 minutes
Sponge Cakes	180–200°C	20–30 minutes
Swiss Rolls	220–230°C	5–7 minutes
Biscuits	170–180°C	12–18 minutes

COOLING

Once the cake or sponge leaves the oven you should allow it to stand in its tin or tray for 5–10 minutes to allow it to settle and become firm. This will avoid it becoming damaged.

If you do not require the cake or sponge straight away, cool then wrap and freeze until required.

BASIC CAKE DECORATING TECHNIQUES

Enrobing is the term used to cover a cake or sponge base with a coating, for example, ganache or fondant.

The cake base is placed on a wire cooling rack which is placed over a dip tray. The coating is poured over the cake base and quickly spread with a palette knife to allow the coating to flow all down the sides; the excess will run directly onto the dip tray. The coating is allowed to set slightly before removing to be finished further. It is important to get the consistency of the coating right. It should evenly coat the back of a wooden spoon when poured over the spoon.

Making and using a paper piping bag This is one of the most difficult tasks of cake decorating to learn, but it can allow you to add those finishing touches to your cake to impress even the most skilled professional baker.

Hold the paper triangle as shown, grasping the centre of the long side between the thumb and forefinger of the left hand.

While still holding the paper, using the right hand, roll the top corner down to the centre of the triangle. Hold the paper in this position with the right hand.

With the left hand, roll the bottom corner up to complete the cone.

Adjust the cone so that the point is completely closed and the point is sharp. Fold the loose edges of the open end of the cone so that it will not unroll.

Fill the cone and fold the open end several times so that the filling doesn't come out. Hold the cone between the thumb and forefinger as shown. Cut off the tip to produce a fine hole.

Apply pressure from the top of the cone and pipe or decorate.

Using a pastry bag and piping tubes allows you to add those finishing touches to that perfect gateau or can be used to fill those light, crisp choux pastry eclairs with freshly whipped cream. There are many designs, borders and inscriptions that can be achieved using a pastry bag fitted with different piping tubes, however, there is one common mistake that many good home bakers make – that is not knowing when to stop decorating. The end result is a heavy, unattractive mess! The message when it comes to finishing is: 'Unless you are very experienced and skilled, keep it simple!'

For those needing to practise filling and using the pastry bag and piping tubes, refer to the Equipment section in this book, under Pastry Bag and Piping Tube, for more details.

CAKE PRODUCT FAULTS

FAULTS / CAUSES	Underbaked	Overbaked	Oven temp too low	Oven temp too high	Excessive sugar	Excessive fat	Excessive baking powder	Excessive flour	Too little baking powder	Knocked entering the oven	Flour too weak	Flour too strong	Batter overmixed	Fruit too wet	Lack of steam in oven	Insufficient sugar	Overcraming batter	Insufficient liquids
Sunken fruit														•			•	
Cake sinking in the middle	•				•	•	•		•								•	
Peaked tops				•				•				•	•		•	•		•
Poor volume	•		•	•	•	•	•	•	•	•	•	•	•	•	•	•		•
Spots on crust					•			•										
Dense texture			•	•		•		•	•	•						•		•
Open texture					•			•									•	
Coarse dry texture		•	•	•				•	•									•
Poor keeping properties		•	•	•				•				•	•		•	•	•	•
Excessive crust colour	•	•		•	•			•							•			

48

ALL ABOUT PASTRIES

Pastry making is a real art. In most recipes the pastry is the vehicle that carries the other flavours and it should have a presence but not be the dominant component.

For bakers in a hurry or for those who have not perfected their pastry skills, there is a range of pastries in the supermarket. Irvines frozen pastries include sweet short pastry, puff pastry, flaky pastry and phyllo pastry in 400–500 g packs. Some pastry can be bought ready rolled, which is very easy and convenient to use. If thawing pastry, take care to thaw it slowly. The best way is to place it in the refrigerator overnight. If in a real hurry, the pre-rolled sheets will thaw at room temperature in under half-an-hour.

BASIC INGREDIENTS

Puff Pastry

There are four basic ingredients used in the manufacture of puff pastry:

- medium or strong flour
- butter or special pastry margarine
- salt
- water

Often the only other ingredients used are lemon juice or cream of tartar.

Short and Sweet Pastry

Short and sweet pastries are made using a completely different manufacturing procedure and this is reflected in the ingredients used:

- standard baker's flour
- butter or margarine
- salt
- sugar (for sweet pastry)
- egg and/or water

Other ingredients used can be cocoa for chocolate sweet pastry, baking powder, lemon zest or vanilla essence for flavour.

Choux Pastry

In the make up stages of choux pastry it is more like a batter than a traditional pastry; however, once cooked, it has all the characteristics of a pastry – light and delicate. Choix pastry contains:

- strong flour
- water
- butter or margarine
- eggs

Choux pastry is the most difficult to make, as it requires skill, experience and understanding to achieve the desired finished product.

BASIC INGREDIENT FUNCTIONS

Listed overleaf are the ingredient functions for all pastry types.

Flour is important because its protein- (gluten) forming potential can dictate the lift that will be obtained, and because it forms the final structure of the pastry. For both puff and choux pastry strong flour should be used, as you require the strength and good quality protein (gluten). In the case of short and sweet pastry a medium or strong flour is suitable due to the high percentage of fat or butter used, which softens and weakens the protein (gluten), allowing the pastry to be more biscuit-like.

Salt improves the flavour and has a strengthening effect upon the protein (gluten) which is required for puff and choux pastry.

Butter or special pastry margarine has different functions in all three pastries.

Puff Pastry: Butter or special pastry margarines are used in the dough stage to make the dough softer and easier to handle. It also makes the finished pastry more tender and shorter to eat. Butter or special pastry margarines are used to separate the layers of dough which influence the degree of lift of the pastry and also have an effect on the eating quality of the baked pastry (this butter or special pastry margarine is often referred to as the layering fat). The amount of layering fat can vary between 50–100 percent based on the flour weight.

In commercial terms we usually define the type of pastry made by the amount of layering fat used:

- Half puff pastry: 50 percent of layering fat based on flour weight
- Three-quarter puff pastry: 75 percent of layering fat based on flour weight
- Full puff pastry: 100 percent of layering fat based on flour weight

Short and sweet pastry Butter or special pastry margarines are used to shorten and weaken the protein (gluten), allowing the pastry to be more biscuit-like (shortbread).

Choux Pastry Butter or special pastry margarines are used to allow the extensible protein (gliadin) to stretch without snapping or breaking when the choux pastry rises in the oven.

Water is largely required to obtain the correct consistency of the dough. Water also hydrates the protein (gluten) and allows it to become elastic and extensible. The amount used depends upon the absorption rate of the flour, the amount of fat used in the dough and the process used.

Sugar is mainly used in the manufacture of sweet pastry, which requires a sweeter tasting finished product. Sugar in conjunction with butter has a softening and shortening effect on the protein (gluten). The higher the sugar percentage, the crispier and more biscuit-like the sweet pastry will be. Caster sugar is always used to ensure the sugar crystals dissolve.

Eggs are generally not used in the manufacture of puff pastry but are essential in choux pastry.

Choux Pastry: Eggs make up the highest percentage in the recipe, approximately 200 percent based on flour weight. It is important that fresh good quality eggs are used as, unlike most recipes where the flour protein (gluten) supplies the structure, in choux pastry the egg protein (albumin) supplies the structure.

Sweet Pastry: Eggs are mainly used to enrich the dough for top quality sweet pastry goods. Eggs also improve the handling qualities of sweet pastry when rolling the pastry thin and pressing into tart moulds, etc.

Baking powder adds lightness and apparent shortness to sweet pastry. In top quality sweet pastry this is not necessary.

Cream of tartar and lemon juice are both acids which have a toughening but mellowing (allowing extensibility) effect on the protein (gluten), resulting in improved volume. If using either one of these acids always ensure you do not use an excessive amount, as this will turn your puff pastry sour and result in a low volume puff pastry. If using good quality flour, the addition of acid is not required.

MIXING AND PROCESSING METHODS

PUFF PASTRY

Once the initial dough has been formed by mixing the flour, chilled water, salt and the dough fat together to achieve a three-quarter developed dough, there are three methods of incorporating the layering fat.

Scotch Method (also known as the blitz, rough puff or all-in method)

1. The layering fat is cut into small cubes and incorporated during the formation of the dough made from flour, chilled water, salt and dough fat.
2. It is essential that the dough is not overmixed at this stage, as the layering fat needs to remain intact.
3. Allow this dough to rest for 5–10 minutes to allow the protein (gluten) to relax.
4. The pastry is now ready to be given its layers (known as the lamination stage).

Scotch puff pastry at the completion of mixing ready for the lamination stage to take place. Note the layering fat still intact.

English Method

1. Once the basic dough of flour, chilled water, salt and dough fat has been made, allow the dough to rest for 5–10 minutes to enable the protein (gluten) to relax.
2. Roll out the dough to a large rectangle approximately 1.5 cm thick.
3. Condition the layering fat so that it is of the same consistency as the dough. Then shape it to cover three-quarters of the rolled out dough. This is often the success or failure of the puff pastry. Ensure the layering fat is not too hard or too soft.
4. Place the conditioned layering fat over three-quarters of the rolled out dough.
5. Fold the uncovered third of dough over the layering fat.
6. Fold the remaining third back over to obtain three layers of dough and two layers of layering fat.
7. The pastry is now ready to be given its layers (known as the lamination stage).

English method, step 4

English method, step 5

English method, step 6

French Method (often known as the envelope method)

1. Once the basic dough of flour, chilled water, salt and dough fat has been made, allow the dough to rest for 5–10 minutes to enable the protein (gluten) to relax.
2. Roll out the dough to a large rectangle approximately 2 cm thick.
3. Condition the layering fat so that it is of the same consistency as the dough. Then shape it to fit inside the rolled out dough. This is often the success or failure of the puff pastry. Ensure the layering fat is not too hard or too soft.

French method, step 4

French method, step 5

4. Place the conditioned layering fat in the centre of the rolled out dough.
5. Fold each corner of the dough into the centre to encase the layering fat in an envelope, obtaining two layers of dough and one layer of layering fat.
6. The pastry is now ready to be given its layers (known as the lamination stage).

The Lamination Process

The method used to incorporate the layering fat into the dough is irrelevant to the lamination process. There are two methods of layering the dough and fat that have been formed. These are commonly referred to as turns or folds. In this procedure we are trying to achieve hundreds of thin layers of fat and dough – in most cases up to 400 layers are formed.

Half Fold: (also known as a 3-fold or half turn)
1. Roll out the pastry to a rectangle 1.25 cm thick.
2. By eye mentally divide the rectangle into thirds.
3. Fold A to C and then D to B to complete three layers of pastry. Rest for 15–20 minutes, covered with a plastic bag to prevent the pastry drying out and skinning.
4. Repeat this process three times.
5. The pastry is either ready to be rolled out to its final thickness for product make-up or to be kept in the refrigerator or freezer until required.

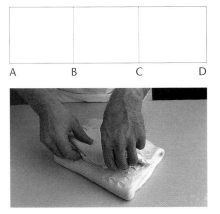

Rolling and folding to achieve a half fold.

Book Fold: (also known as a 4-fold or full turn)
1. Roll out the pastry to a rectangle 1.25 cm thick.
2. By eye mentally divide the rectangle into half.
3. Fold A to B and then C to B. Then fold the whole pastry in half again to complete four layers of pastry. Rest for 15–20 minutes, covered with a plastic bag to prevent the pastry drying out and skinning
4. Repeat this process twice more.
5. The pastry is either ready to be rolled out to its final thickness for product make-up or to be kept in the refrigerator or freezer until required.

Rolling and folding to achieve a book fold.

Points to consider when processing puff pastry

1. Always adhere to the resting times stated to avoid shrinkage in the finished baked product.
2. When rolling and folding your puff pastry, use as little dusting flour as possible, brushing away any excess flour before completing each fold.
3. When making puff pastry ensure that all your ingredients are kept cool.
4. During resting periods keep the pastry covered with plastic and keep cool in the refrigerator.
5. Always rest your puff pastry products before baking – the longer the better (anywhere from 2–12 hours in the refrigerator). Allow to warm up before baking.
6. When rolling out for each fold, ensure that the open ends are folded back into the dough.
7. Always ensure that your dough and layering fat are the same consistency when incorporating the layering fat.

8. Always use chilled water. In the summer you need to use iced chilled water (do not put the ice cubes in the dough, as they will not dissolve during mixing).

How does puff pastry rise?

1. Once the hundreds of layers of dough and layering fat enter the oven (the oven must be at the correct temperature) the fat melts and the moisture within the dough begins to produce steam.
2. The protein (gluten) in the dough layers begins to expand.
3. The steam pushes the dough layers upwards.
4. Once the puff pastry has reached its maximum volume and all the moisture within has escaped, the protein (gluten) begins to coagulate (set), giving it its structure.
5. If the puff pastry is taken out of the oven before complete coagulation (setting), the structure will collapse.

Storage of puff pastry

Unbaked puff pastry can be stored in the refrigerator or freezer in block or rolled form. Thaw your puff pastry in the refrigerator overnight, then let it stand at room temperature for approximately 30 minutes.

Baking guidelines

This is a general guide to baking puff pastry. All times and temperatures are guides only and will vary from oven to oven.

PRODUCT	TEMPERATURE	TIME (VARIABLE)
Unfilled puff pastry	220–230°C	18–20 minutes
Filled puff pastry (sweet)	215–220°C	20–25 minutes
Filled puff pastry (savoury)	220–225°C	25–30 minutes
Reheating puff pastry products	190–200°C	15–25 minutes

Cooling

Puff pastry should be cooled on a cooling rack to avoid sweating. Pies should be allowed to cool slightly before being removed from their tins. This will stop the pie from collapsing.

SHORT AND SWEET PASTRY

The main difference between short and sweet pastry is the amount of sugar used. There are four methods of making short and sweet pastry, but the two most common methods are the creaming and blending.

Creaming Method

1. Beat the butter, salt and sugar until light, creamy and fluffy.

2. Continue beating on low speed while adding the liquid or egg.
3. Slowly mix in the dry ingredients and mix until a clear, smooth paste is formed. Do not overmix.
4. The pastry is ready for processing.

Blending Method

1. Mix the butter and flour together until no lumps are left and the mix resembles ground almonds or a crumble.
2. Mix liquid or eggs with the sugar and salt, then slowly add to the dry mixture while mixing on a slow speed.
3. Mix until a clear, smooth paste is formed. Do not overmix.
4. The pastry is ready for processing.

Creating shortness in short and sweet pastry

The mixing methods that are used in making short and sweet pastry are designed to coat the flour particles with fat, thus protecting the development of the protein (gluten) network when the liquids are added. Mixing this way will always ensure that a short, tender pastry is obtained. Of course this is only achieved in conjunction with the correct mixing time.

Points to consider when processing short and sweet pastry

1. Do not overmix.
2. Avoid excessive handling of the pastry.
3. Work in a cool environment.

Storage of short and sweet pastry

Unbaked short and sweet pastry can be stored in the refrigerator and freezer, unfilled or filled. It is advisable to thaw your short or sweet pastry out in the refrigerator overnight, then let it stand at room temperature for approximately 30 minutes.

Baking guidelines

This is a general guide to baking short and sweet pastry. All times and temperatures are guides only and will vary from oven to oven.

PRODUCT	TEMPERATURE	TIME (VARIABLE)
Unfilled short pastry	200–220°C	18–20 minutes
Filled short pastry	215–220°C	20–25 minutes
Unfilled sweet pastry	180–190°C	18–20 minutes
Filled sweet pastry	180–190°C	25–30 minutes
Reheating short and sweet pastry products	180–190°C	15–25 minutes

Cooling

Baked short or sweet pastry should be cooled on a cooling rack to avoid sweating. Pies

A flan tin being lined with sweet pastry before being filled.

should be allowed to cool slightly before being removed from their tins. This will stop the pie collapsing.

CHOUX PASTRY

One of the secrets to top quality choux pastries is cooking the roux or base and knowing how much egg to add. There is only one method of producing choux pastry.

General Method

1. Boil the water and butter, then remove from the heat.
2. Add the strong flour and return to a medium heat. Cook this basic roux for 4–5 minutes, stirring all the time. Avoid overcooking the roux as this will dry it out.
3. Allow the roux to cool slightly before adding the eggs in small additions. Beat well between each addition.
4. Add enough egg to hold 'soft peaks'.
5. Place into a piping bag with a tube attached and pipe onto a greased tray.
6. Bake in a hot oven (210–225°C). Do not open the door for the first 15–20 minutes.

Choux pastry ready to be piped. Notice the consistency of the batter.

Points to consider when processing choux pastry

1. Always use strong flour.
2. Do not leave the water and butter boiling too long, as some of the water will evaporate.
3. Always use fresh eggs.
4. Do not overcook the roux.
5. Ensure you add the correct amount of egg, beating well between each small addition. The egg amounts will always be variable.
6. Always bake in a hot oven.
7. Never open the oven door too early, as this will allow the steam to escape.

What causes choux pastry to rise?

1. The choux pastry enters the oven as a thick, shiny mass.
2. Once steam is produced from the water within the batter, it pushes upwards causing the choux pastry to 'balloon' and rise.
3. Once the pastry has risen to its maximum height and the moisture from the batter has escaped, the protein (albumin) present within the eggs will coagulate (set), giving the choux pastry strength and structure.
4. At this stage, the choux pastry must be given time to dry out, otherwise the proteins inside will not support the outer shell, and it will collapse upon cooling.

Baking guidelines

This is a general guide to baking choux pastry. All times and temperatures are guides only and will vary from oven to oven.

PRODUCT	TEMPERATURE	TIME (VARIABLE)
Choux pastry	220–225°C	20–25 minutes (drying time 5 minutes)

Storage of choux pastry

Unbaked choux pastry should be baked fresh straight away. It is common practice to freeze baked choux pastry, which only requires thawing before use. Some bakers place the thawed choux pastry in a warm oven for a few minutes to dry any moisture collected during freezing.

Cooling

Once the choux pastry has been baked, place directly onto cooling wire. This will allow air circulation and prevent the product sweating.

FAULTS IN PUFF PASTRY

FAULTS \ CAUSES	Incorrect rolling technique	Fat too hard	Too short rest before baking	Uneven oven heat	Too many turns/folds	Rolled out too thin	Flour used was too weak	Layering fat too soft	Room temp too warm	Too much fat used	Not enough fat used	Oven temp too low	Incorrect cutting out	Tough layering fat used	Too strong flour used	Dough made too tight	Dough made too slack	Skinning of pastry	Poor sealing	Insufficient turns/folds	Pastry left uncovered
Uneven lift	•	•	•	•									•					•	•	•	
Poor volume	•				•	•	•	•	•	•	•	•	•			•	•	•			
Distorted shape	•		•	•									•					•		•	
Shrinkage			•												•	•	•				
Fat seepage during baking		•						•		•										•	
Tough eating					•						•			•	•	•	•	•			
Filling spilling out			•										•					•			
Skinning																					•

FAULTS IN SHORT AND SWEET PASTRY PRODUCTS

FAULTS \ CAUSES	Not enough fat, egg, sugar	Too strong flour used	Too little egg/liquid used	Too much egg/liquid used	Not rested before baking	Too much aeration	Too much sugar	Oven temp too high	Oven temp too low	Too much fat used	Overmixed	Undermixed	Too much filling
Tough pastry	•	•	•	•							•		
Shrinkage	•	•		•	•						•		
Distort shape	•	•		•	•						•		
Dense texture	•	•	•								•		
Dark in colour							•	•					
Lack of colour	•								•				
Pastry breaking, too short						•	•			•		•	
Brown spot on the crust							•						
Filling boiling out during baking													•

BORDEAUX BAKERY

Genuine French breads and pastries are baked by this passionate, authentic French baker in his busy bakery and café on bustling Thorndon Quay in the heart of Wellington. Out the back, the bakery is filled with linen baskets, enormous ovens and mixers, and shelves are crammed with special sugars, fruit purées and special patisserie moulds. Jean Louis hails from Bordeaux and is genuinely pleased with the success he has found in New Zealand.

'Customers drive from the Wairarapa and all over the Wellington region to buy my bread,' he boasts, 'but it would have taken two generations in France to have built a business to this size!'

The shelves of his shop are filled with a full range of such specialities as baguettes, boules, rustic breads, couronne, and such delicate patisserie as canèles, the tiny treats from Bordeaux that are almost custard-like in their interior. Jean Louis remains French in his loyalty, and sources baking equipment, machinery, ingredients and, above all, authentic recipes directly from France. His love for the art of baking is evident as he explains that he makes bread with his heart, and that a baker must have total 'feel' for his dough, adding something of his passion to every loaf.

Brioches

A classic French bread, brioche is a light yeast-baked sweet bread that is perfect for toasting or simply buttering when fresh, soft and airy. Brioche is also the base for many French desserts and it is the most perfect bread to use in a good old-fashioned bread and butter pudding.

1. Sieve the flour onto your work surface. Make a well and add the salt, sugar and yeast.
2. Slowly add the water and three-quarters of the egg, knead the dough for 6–7 minutes or until the dough is almost fully developed (it is important to develop the gluten structure before all the egg is added).
3. Continue to add the balance of the egg slowly while the dough is still being kneaded. Add sufficient egg to achieve a very soft, elastic, very smooth and shiny dough.
4. While kneading, slowly add the softened butter in small amounts. Knead in all the butter to achieve a smooth, elastic, silky dough. Do not overmix the dough as this will cause overheating and the dough will become oily and greasy.
5. Transfer the dough into a lightly oiled container covered with plastic wrap; give a bulk fermentation time of one hour in a warm draught-free place. The dough should double in size.
6. Gently knock back the dough to expel all the gases, reactivate the yeast and strengthen the gluten structure. Finally, push the dough out to a thickness of 5 cm, place into a shallow container, then cover with plastic wrap.
7. Place in the refrigerator overnight (12 hours). This makes the dough easier to mould since the dough will be cold and firm.
8. The following day, scale off into 300 g and 50 g pieces for large brioches or 50 and 10 g pieces for small brioches. Mould both pieces into round shapes, flatten the larger ball slightly and make a hole in the middle with your finger; then place it into a greased brioche mould.
9. Mould the smaller ball into a tear drop and push it into the hole of the larger ball firmly with your fingers. Alternatively, place six 70 g round balls inside a greased bread tin (three each side).
10. Cover and prove in a warm, draught-free place until double in size (2–3 hours).
11. Using a pastry brush, gently glaze with egg wash.
12. Place directly into a preheated oven at 210°C for 12–15 minutes or until golden brown.
13. Remove from the moulds after 10 minutes and place on a wire cooling rack.

Variations

You can roll chocolate pieces or fruit fillings into the centre of the brioche at step 8, if desired. Process as for standard brioche.

500 g Champion or Elfin High Grade Flour
10 g salt
50 g granulated sugar
8 g Elfin Dried Yeast (1 sachet)
50 ml water
350 g eggs (7) (variable)
250 g softened butter

Finished dough temperature: 27°C

Croissants

An infinite amount of care and patience is needed to achieve the perfect croissant. There is nothing quite like a warm croissant, flaky and light and served with a steaming bowl of milky coffee.

DOUGH

500 g Champion or Elfin High
  Grade Flour (chilled in the
  refrigerator overnight)
15 g gluten flour
10 g salt
50 g sugar
8 g Elfin Dried Yeast (1 sachet)
egg wash for finishing
140 ml chilled water (placed in the
  refrigerator overnight)
130 ml chilled milk

Finished dough temperature: 15°C

LAYERING FAT

280 g butter (if using special butter
  sheets delete the flour below)
50 g Champion or Elfin High
  Grade Flour

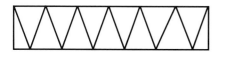

1. Sieve the flour and gluten onto your work surface. Make a well and add the salt, sugar, yeast, milk and water.

2. Mix or knead the dough by hand using the technique shown in the All About Bread section. Continue to knead the dough by hand. Every couple of minutes stop and check the gluten development and temperature of the dough. Only half develop your dough. This should take 5–7 minutes. At this stage the dough should be firm and cold.

3. Place the dough in a floured bowl. Cover with plastic and rest for 45 minutes in a warm, draught-free place. While the dough is resting prepare the layering fat by placing the butter and flour into a mixing bowl fitted with a beater. Mix together on a low speed until it forms a solid mass. Don't overmix or soften the butter too much. Place the layering fat between two layers of plastic and roll out to a flat square 17 cm x 17 cm. Place in the refrigerator to firm up.

4. Gently knock back the dough, place back into the bowl and cover. Rest in the refrigerator for 3 hours.

5. Incorporate the layering fat into the dough using the French Method (see Mixing and Processing in the All About Pastries section). Ensure the dough is kept cool during the make up of croissants.

6. You should now have an envelope of dough with the layering fat inside. Carefully roll out the dough on a lightly floured board lengthways to achieve a rectangle 10–15 mm in thickness. Give a half fold (see the Laminating Process in the All About Pastries section). Place on a floured tray, wrap in plastic and place in the freezer for 5 minutes.

7. Remove from the freezer and repeat the above process.

8. You should have now given the croissant dough three half folds. Rest the dough for 15 minutes in the freezer.

9. Remove from the freezer and gradually roll the dough out on a floured surface to a rectangle shape of 80 cm wide x 20 cm long and 4 mm thick, ensuring that the pastry is freely moving during the rolling process. Keep the pastry as rectangular and as even as possible. Trim the outside edges.

10. Using a large chef's knife cut the rectangle into even triangles (see diagram, left). Average triangle size is 8 cm wide x 15 cm long.

11. Roll each triangle up starting at the base and rolling and stretching to the bottom, bend and pinch the ends on each other to form a crescent shape.

12. Place onto a greased or baking paper lined baking tray.

13. Cover with plastic and place in a warm place to proof for 45 minutes or until almost double in size.

14. After proofing, very gently brush the croissants with egg wash (two parts egg to one part milk or water).

15. Place directly into a preheated oven set at 220°C and bake for 15–18 minutes until golden brown.

16. Place onto a wire cooling rack.

Paris Brest

Filled with a rich, creamy French custard, this delicate choux pastry ring is a classic gateau found throughout France. Take care to read the notes on choux pastry in the All About Pastries section before commencing. Paris Brest makes a stunning dessert or can be an excellent accompaniment to coffee.

PASTRY

125 ml cold water

pinch of salt

75 g butter

105 g Champion or Elfin High Grade Flour

175 g eggs (3$^1/_2$) (variable)

40 g flaked almond

icing sugar to dust

FILLING

250 ml milk

2–3 drops vanilla essence

65 g granulated sugar

75 g eggs (1$^1/_2$)

35 g Champion or Elfin Standard Plain Flour

5 g cornflour

20 g butter

300 g whipped cream (sweetened)

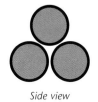

Side view

1. Place the water, salt and butter in a saucepan and bring to the boil. Remove from the heat.
2. Add the flour and mix in using a wooden spoon until well combined.
3. Return to a low heat and cook the basic roux for 2 minutes, stirring all the time to avoid the mixture sticking to the bottom. This will slightly dry the mixture out.
4. Place in a mixing bowl, and beat to cool the mixture.
5. Slowly add the eggs (almost one by one) beating well between each addition (all of the eggs may not be required).
6. The mixture should not be runny; it should hold soft peaks or when the spoon is run through the mixture the trench walls will remain standing for approximately 10 seconds before collapsing in on themselves.
7. Place the mixture in a piping bag fitted with a 1 cm piping tube.
8. On a lightly greased and floured baking tray, trace a 10 cm round circle. This choux pastry is enough to do two 10 cm Paris Brest.
9. Pipe a ring of choux paste around the circle.
10. Pipe another circle inside the first one so that it is just touching the side.
11. Finally pipe a third circle on top and in the middle of the two bottom circles (see diagram).
12. Using a pastry brush, lightly egg wash the choux paste, then very lightly scrape the top with a fork to give a decorative pattern.
13. Sprinkle the top with flaked almonds.
14. Place into a preheated oven set at 230°C and bake for 20 minutes before checking. Ensure that you do not open the oven door during this first 20 minutes, as this will cause the choux paste to collapse.
15. Reduce the heat to 200°C and open the oven door. Continue to bake the choux for another 15–20 minutes or until the choux paste has dried out.
16. Place directly onto a wire cooling rack and cool completely.
17. To assemble, slice the choux paste ring in half horizontally, and carefully remove the top half. Using a piping bag fitted with a star piping tube, pipe the crème diplomat filling (see recipe below) around the ring.
18. Replace the top half of the choux paste ring and place onto a serving plate.
19. Dust lightly with icing sugar before serving.

Crème Diplomat Filling

1. Place the milk, vanilla essence and half the sugar in a saucepan. Stir and bring to the boil.
2. Meanwhile in a bowl whisk the egg and the remaining sugar until the mixture becomes pale yellow and thick.
3. Sieve the flour and cornflour together and slowly add this to the egg and sugar mixture while still whisking to avoid any lumps. Do not overmix.
4. Once the milk and sugar mixture has come to the boil, add half of this to the

sugar/egg and flour batter. Stir constantly with a whisk.

5. Return this mixture to the remaining milk in the saucepan and whisk together to stop any lumps forming.

6. Place on a low heat and cook the mixture until it thickens, stirring all the time. Increase the heat, bring to the boil and cook for 3 minutes while still stirring.

7. Remove from the heat and whisk in the butter.

8. Transfer into a bowl and cover with plastic wrap. Cool completely before using – this is important.

9. Fold the whipped cream into the cold cream patisserie in several additions, ensuring that they are well combined.

10. Use immediately.

French Baguettes and Boules

This is Jean Louis' recipe for pâté à pain, the basic French bread dough that is shaped into crisp baguettes or the more substantial round white boules. These breads are the mainstay of every French bakery and these are the loaves that customers seek from far and wide. In fact, many connoisseurs agree that Bordeaux Bakery produces the best French bread in New Zealand.

500 g Champion or Elfin High
   Grade Flour
10 g gluten flour
5 g Elfin Dried Yeast
300 g cold water
10 g salt
rye flour to dust

Finished dough temperature: 25°C

1. Sieve the flour onto your work surface. Make a well and add the gluten and yeast.
2. Slowly add the water to the well.
3. Mix or knead the dough by hand using the technique shown in the All About Bread section. Continue kneading until the ingredients are well combined, 3–4 minutes (the dough is not fully developed at this stage).
4. Put the dough in a bowl, and cover with plastic. Leave the dough for 10 minutes to rest.
5. Add the salt.
6. Continue to knead the dough by hand. Every couple of minutes stop and check the gluten development and temperature of the dough. This final kneading should take about 15 minutes (check if you have fully developed the dough by using the stretch test). It is important to ensure that the dough is fully developed for this bread.
7. Lightly oil a bowl large enough to allow the dough to double in bulk. Put the dough in the bowl and cover with plastic. Leave in a warmish place (23–25°C) for 30 minutes. By this time the dough should be nearly double in size.
8. Gently knock back the dough in the bowl. This will deflate it slightly, but will develop more strength. Cover again and leave for 60 minutes, then knock it back again. After resting in the bowl for another 30–40 minutes the dough should be fully fermented.
9. Tip the dough out onto a lightly floured bench and, using a dough scraper, cut the dough into 200 g for baguettes and 450 g for boules. Be gentle with the dough – do not aggressively punch it down, or squeeze all the gas from within. Pick each piece up and gently tuck the edges underneath, pulling the surface tight around the mass. Lay the pieces back on the floured bench and cover with a proofing cloth (or tea towel). Give an intermediate proof of 10 minutes. While you wait, lightly dust a proofing cloth or tea towel with rye flour.
10. Uncover the dough and mould each piece into a baguette or boule shape. For the baguette, flatten the dough piece out as for rolling up a swiss roll, then tightly roll the dough towards you as you would for a swiss roll, applying pressure with your hands as you roll; the tighter the roll the better. For the boule, shape each piece into a ball by cupping your hands around the dough and moving it in a circular motion, pulling the skin tight over the dough. Don't overdo it though, or the skin will rip and this will spoil the appearance of the finished product. The final shape will look like a smooth ball, but with a rough, scrunched-up bottom.

11. Place the baguettes on a proofing cloth dusted with rye flour, remembering to leave a pleat between each baguette, or place seam side down in special baguette trays. For the boules place the ball top surface down into a round proofing basket or bowl lined with calico dusted with rye flour.

12. Final proof for approximately 35–45 minutes in a warm, draught-free place. Cover with plastic to prevent skinning and chilling of the dough. Use the indentation test to tell when the dough is three-quarters proofed. Do not overproof.

13. The oven should be preheated to 240–250°C, with a baking stone in place. Gently tip one loaf out onto a peel lightly dusted with semolina. Using a razor blade or sharp knife, slash four deep 45° cuts in the top of the baguette and four cuts vertically and horizontally (trellis) for the boule (see diagrams).

14. Just before you load the bread into the oven, spray water into the oven cavity. Close the door quickly so you don't lose any of the steam.

15. With the peel and loaf in one hand, open the oven with the other, and gently 'flick' the baguettes or boules off the peel and onto the baking stone. Close the oven door immediately.

16. Bake for 20 minutes, then turn the heat down to 210°C, and check the loaves for even baking. If necessary, turn them around. For the remaining time leave the door of the oven slightly ajar to thicken and dry the crust.

17. After a total of 30–35 minutes the loaves will be ready. Cool on a wire rack.

CITY CAKE COMPANY

With a clean, slick New York feel to its two retail outlets, the City Cake Company has very quickly found a niche market in Auckland for specialty individualised cakes. There are three partners in this thriving business: Maureen Keene, her daughter Tracy Baird, and Susanna Pattisson. Surprisingly none are involved in hands-on baking but all definitely have a hand in product conception and development, and provide a strong business base.

The main focus is superbly presented cakes that taste as good as they look. Baking is done in a busy factory in an Auckland suburb by a team of bakers who produce cakes for the retail shops and for customers who seek specially designed wedding and occasion cakes. The team is totally committed to cakes baked with the best ingredients, and the business was founded on Maureen Keene's desire to bake cakes 'that tasted fabulous'.

It can take weeks to develop a new idea to the point where a cake is ready for marketing, and it is then showcased through the retail shops. City Cake Company offers a constantly changing 'menu' of cakes to be eaten by the slice with coffee, or taken home to be savoured at smart dinner parties and special events.

Greek Coconut Cake

With a wonderful lemony syrup and almost crunchy coconut topping, this cake is particularly moreish and decidedly moist.

1. Place the butter and sugar in a mixing bowl fitted with a beater.
2. Beat until the butter and sugar just begin to change colour (do not cream).
3. Add the eggs, coconut and flour in five additions: starting with the egg, then the coconut and lastly the flour, repeating until each is mixed in. Beat well between each addition to ensure the mixture does not curdle.
4. Place the batter into a 20 cm round, loose bottomed spring release cake tin that has been prepared lightly greased and lined on the bottom and sides with greaseproof paper. This is necessary to avoid overbaking due to the long baking time required.
5. Place directly into a preheated oven set at 150°C and bake for 2–2$\frac{1}{2}$ hours. Insert a cake skewer in the centre of the cake, and if it comes out clean then the cake is baked.
6. Allow to cool in the tin for 30–40 minutes, then using a cake skewer prick 60–70 holes in the top of the cake and evenly pour over the syrup (see recipe below).
7. Immediately spread the coconut topping (see recipe below) evenly over the top.
8. Preheat the oven to 190°C and place the cake back into the oven to bake the coconut topping. Bake until golden brown.
9. Allow the cake to cool in the tin for 20–30 minutes then carefully remove the cake from the tin. Carefully remove the greaseproof paper while still warm.

Syrup
1. Place the sugar, water and lemon or orange quarters in a saucepan.
2. Bring to the boil, stirring occasionally to ensure the sugar is dissolved.
3. Remove from the heat and pass through a sieve.
4. Cool for 30–45 minutes before use.

Coconut Topping
1. Place the brown sugar and cream in a saucepan.
2. Bring to the boil, stirring to dissolve the sugar and avoiding burning.
3. Remove from the heat and stir in the coconut. Use while still warm.

CAKE
240 g softened butter
460 g granulated sugar
450 g eggs (9)
345 g fine coconut
315 g Champion or Elfin Self Rising Flour

SYRUP
275 g granulated sugar
300 ml water
$\frac{1}{2}$ lemon or orange (cut in half again)

TOPPING
165 g soft brown sugar
240 ml fresh cream
165 g shredded coconut

Carrot Cake

Moist, delicious carrot cake is a favourite with young and old. This is especially good for those who have allergies to dairy products as the cake is kept moist with oil. Be sure to use a fresh, light oil such as grapeseed or light olive oil.

CAKE

250 g Champion or Elfin Standard
    Plain Flour

10 g baking soda

5 g salt

5 g mixed spice

5 g cinnamon

200 g eggs (4)

165 g soft brown sugar

290 g granulated sugar

370 g oil

200 g grated carrot

120 g walnut pieces

135 g crushed pineapple (well-drained)

ICING

105 g cream cheese

90 g softened butter

190 g icing sugar (sieved)

1 tablespoon lemon zest

1. Sieve the flour, baking soda, salt, mixed spice and cinnamon into a mixing bowl fitted with a beater.
2. Add the eggs, brown sugar, granulated sugar, oil, carrot, walnut pieces and pineapple to the mixing bowl.
3. Beat on a slow speed for 1 minute then scrape down the sides of the bowl. Beat for a further 2 minutes on a medium speed.
4. Pour the batter into a 20 cm round, loose bottomed spring release cake tin that has been prepared lightly greased and lined on the bottom and sides with greaseproof paper. This is necessary to avoid overbaking due to the long baking time required.
5. Place directly into a preheated oven set at 150°C and bake for $1\frac{1}{2}$–2 hours. Insert a cake skewer in the centre of the cake, and if it comes out clean the cake is baked.
6. Allow to cool in the tin for 30 minutes, then remove from the tin and allow to cool completely. Remove the greaseproof paper.
7. Once the cake is cold, spread the cream cheese icing (see recipe below) on the top using a palette knife. Ensure the icing is smooth and evenly spread.
8. Sprinkle a ring of whole or pecan pieces on top of the icing approximately 2 cm from the edge of the cake.

Cream Cheese Icing

1. Place the cream cheese, butter, icing sugar and lemon zest in a mixing bowl fitted with a beater.
2. Beat on medium speed until the icing is white and fluffy.
3. Use immediately or store in a covered bowl until required. Keeps for 2–3 days.

Summer Fruit Tart – with Lemon Cream

This is quite spectacular when made at the height of the summer berry season, using the colourful combination of as many berries as possible. If you wish to make it in the winter, you could always try topping it with freshly sliced oranges.

PASTRY

170 g salted butter

85 g sugar

50 g egg (1)

260 g Champion or Elfin Standard Plain Flour

FILLING

500 g granulated sugar

1 heaped tablespoon lemon zest

250 ml fresh lemon juice

450 g eggs (9)

2 egg yolks

330 g softened butter

TOPPING

fresh, seasonal fruits, e.g., raspberries, blackberries, cherries, gooseberries, strawberries (glazed), grapes, blueberries, etc.

clotted cream to serve

Sweet Pastry Base

1. Lightly cream the butter and sugar in a mixing bowl fitted with a beater or beat in a bowl with a wooden spoon.
2. Add the egg and mix until combined.
3. Lastly add the flour and mix to a paste. Only mix until the paste comes clean off the bowl. Be careful not to overmix or the pastry will become too elastic and doughy.
4. Transfer to a bowl. Cover and refrigerate for 30 minutes or overnight.
5. On a lightly floured workbench roll the pastry out into a sheet about 5 mm thick, and big enough to cover a 23 cm greased fluted loose bottomed tin.
6. Use the rolling pin to pick the pastry up and lay it over the tin. Gently press the pastry into the tin so that it fills all the contours. Be careful not to stretch the pastry or it will tear, or shrink back in the oven. Return it to the fridge for another 30 minutes, or more if the pastry still feels soft. Reserve the scraps.
7. Preheat the oven to 150°C. Line the pastry with tinfoil and fill with dried beans, raw rice or pastry weights.
8. Bake the pastry for 30 minutes. The pastry should be baked but not coloured.
9. Allow the pastry to cool before checking for any cracks or holes. Also make sure the pastry has not shrunk on the sides. Patch any low points, holes or cracks with your leftover pastry. Return to the oven to bake these patches.
10. Pour the freshly made warm lemon cream filling (see recipe below) into the baked pastry case.
11. Place the filled tart in the refrigerator and allow the filling to set (approximately 2 hours).
12. Cover with fruits of your choice.
13. Serve with fresh clotted cream.

Lemon Cream Filling

1. Place the sugar and lemon zest in a saucepan and rub together with the palms of your hands to infuse the sugar with lemon.
2. Add the lemon juice, eggs, egg yolks and butter. Whisk together to combine.
3. Heat until the mixture just reaches boiling point, stirring constantly with a wooden spoon. Do not boil rapidly or the eggs will scramble.
4. Pour into the baked pastry case immediately.

COPENHAGEN BAKERY

John Thomsen learnt the art of baking in an apprenticeship in Kloster, a tiny town on Denmark's west coast. He and his New Zealand wife Donna have a thriving bakery in the heart of central Christchurch, which is like a home away from home for Danish tourists who regularly gather to taste authentic Danish baking. There's even a guest book that Danes (having heard about the bakery in Australia, China or Bali) sign with sentimental comments, praising the hospitality.

The Thomsens' hard work has seen them purchase a traditional Kiwi bakery and build up such a following that they now have a highly successful retail outlet in the city and an offsite bakery in Bromley where the cakes, bread and pastries are baked. There has been a little compromise to cater for the Kiwi taste, but the rye bread, the pastries and the rund stykker, or fresh crusty bread rolls, are just as they are in Denmark.

'Baking is my life,' says this dedicated baker, who is ably assisted by Donna. Even their two sons, aged six and nine, are showing an interest in baking. Their idea of a treat is to spend a night 'helping' in the bakery, up to their elbows in flour and dough. Copenhagen Bakery's success is in the total family commitment and the philosophy that their shop is a stage where good service is paramount.

Danish Pastries

With their light pastry and sweet delicious fillings, true Danish pastries have grabbed the imagination of people all over the world. The range of Danish pastries in the Copenhagen Bakery makes a fabulous display and they are one of the fastest selling lines.

Dough

1. Sieve the flour onto your work surface. Make a well and add the gluten, salt, sugar, butter, egg, yeast and water.
2. Mix or knead the dough by hand using the technique shown in the All About Bread section. Every couple of minutes stop and check the gluten development and temperature of the dough. Only half develop your dough. This should take 5–7 minutes. At this stage the dough should be firm and cold.
3. Place the dough in a floured bowl. Cover with plastic and rest for 5 minutes in the refrigerator. While the dough is resting prepare the layering fat by placing the butter and flour into a mixing bowl fitted with a beater. Mix together on low speed until it forms a solid mass. Don't overmix or soften the butter too much. Place the layering fat between two layers of plastic and roll out to a flat square 17 cm x 17 cm. Place in the refrigerator to firm up.
4. Remove the dough from the refrigerator (at this stage the yeast within the dough should not be gassing). Incorporate the layering fat into the dough using the French Method (see Mixing and Processing in the All About Pastries section). Ensure the dough is kept cool during the make up of Danish pastries.
5. You should now have an envelope of dough with the layering fat inside. Carefully roll out the dough on a lightly floured board lengthways to achieve a rectangle 15 mm in thickness. Give a half fold (see the laminating process in the All About Pastries section). Place on a floured tray, wrap in plastic and place in the freezer for 5 minutes.
6. Remove from the freezer and repeat the above process twice.
7. You should now give the Danish pastry three half folds, then rest the pastry for 15 minutes in the freezer.
8. Remove from the freezer and gradually roll the pastry out on a floured surface to 4 mm thick, ensuring that the pastry is freely moving during the rolling process. Keep the pastry as square and as even as possible. Trim the outside edges.
9. Cut the pastry into 10 cm x 10 cm. Fill each square with 15 g of butter filling (see recipe on next page).
10. Fold each corner into the middle over the filling. Press firmly to hold down the ends (see photo opposite).
11. Place onto a greased tray or baking paper lined tray.
12. Cover the Danish lightly with a sheet of plastic.
13. Place in a warm place to proof for 45 minutes or until almost double in size.
14. After proofing, very gently brush the pastries with egg wash (two parts egg to one part milk or water). Push down the middle of each pastry with four fingers.

DOUGH
500 g Champion or Elfin High Grade Flour (chilled in the refrigerator overnight)
15 g gluten flour
5 g salt
30 g sugar
60 g butter
100 g eggs (2) (cold)
16 g Elfin Dried Yeast (2 sachets)
200 ml chilled water (ice in the refrigerator overnight)
egg wash for finishing

Finished dough temperature: 15°C

LAYERING FAT
500 g butter (if using special butter sheets delete the flour)
100 g Champion or Elfin High Grade Flour

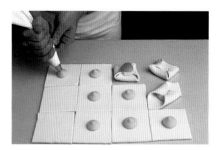

BUTTER FILLING

110 g softened butter

155 g sugar

10 g ground almonds

15 g apricot jam

10 g white cake crumbs

CUSTARD

150 ml milk

20 g sugar

50 ml milk

20 g Edmonds Custard Powder

ICING

400 g icing sugar

140 ml stock syrup (boil 100 ml hot water and 75 g sugar. Cool before use)

15. Fill the middle by piping one of the following into it: jam, thickened fruit filling, lemon curd, custard (see recipe below), fresh or well-drained tinned apricot halves.
16. Place directly into a preheated oven set at 210°C. Bake for 15–18 minutes until golden brown.
17. Cool and brush with apricot glaze (see recipe for Mediterranean Orange Cake, page 119).
18. Drizzle with white icing (see recipe below).

Butter Filling

Mix all the ingredients in a bowl with a wooden spoon until soft, creamy and smooth.

Custard

1. In a saucepan place the first amount of milk and sugar. Stir and bring to the boil.
2. Mix the second amount of milk with the custard powder in a bowl.
3. Add the boiled milk to the custard mix, then pour into the saucepan and return to a medium heat to thicken.
4. Cool before use.

White Water Icing

Sieve icing sugar and add stock syrup. You may have to warm it slightly to achieve the correct thickish, runny consistency.

Dream Biscuits

A simple yet delicious biscuit that is superb served with coffee. Coffee drinking is an important part of Danish culture and tourists find their way to the Copenhagen Bakery for a little relaxation and a taste of home.

1. Place the butter in a mixing bowl and soften in the microwave on a low heat. Attach a beater and mix all the ingredients together. Don't overmix. If the dough becomes too soft, wrap in plastic wrap and place in the refrigerator.
2. On a lightly floured surface, roll out the biscuit dough to a thickness of 6–7 mm. Keep the dough rectangular. Trim the edges to keep even.
3. Using a palette knife spread a thin layer of royal icing (see below) on the top of the dough, approximately 2 mm thick.
4. Sprinkle with flaked almonds. Let the royal icing (see recipe below) dry before cutting (approximately 1–2 hours).
5. Using a sharp cook's knife carefully cut the dough into 3 cm x 3 cm squares.
6. Slide your palette knife underneath each square of dough, then transfer onto a baking tray lined with baking paper. Allow 1–2 cm between each biscuit.
7. Place directly into a preheated oven set at 180°C. Bake until golden brown, for 10–15 minutes.

Royal Icing

1. Mix the icing sugar in a stainless steel mixing bowl with a wooden spoon.
2. Beat together with 2–3 drops of lemon juice. Beat until stiff and spreadable.
3. Cover to prevent drying out during use.

BISCUITS
375 g butter
150 g caster sugar
475 g Champion or Elfin Standard
   Plain Flour

TOPPING
natural flaked almonds
royal icing (see recipe below)

ICING
350 g icing sugar
2 egg whites
lemon juice

Honey and Almond Tart

Prepared ahead, this tart would make a sweet ending to a dinner party. Serve it with coffee, as a dessert or as a special afternoon tea cake.

PASTRY

170 g salted butter

85 g sugar

50 g egg (1)

260 g Champion or Elfin Standard
  Plain Flour

FILLING

75g butter

75 g granulated sugar

50 g ground almonds

25 g golden syrup

75 g eggs (1½) (warmed)

25 g Champion or Elfin Standard Plain
  Flour

1–2 drops almond essence

TOPPING

50 g liquid honey

500 g sugar

25 g fresh cream

25 g flaked almonds

1. Lightly cream the butter and sugar in a mixing bowl fitted with a beater or beat in a bowl with a wooden spoon.
2. Add the egg and mix until combined.
3. Lastly add the flour and mix to a paste. Only mix until the paste comes clean off the bowl. Be careful not to overmix or the pastry will become too elastic and doughy.
4. Transfer to a bowl. Cover and refrigerate for 30 minutes or overnight.
5. On a lightly floured workbench roll the pastry out into a sheet about 5 mm thick, and big enough to cover an 18 cm greased, loose bottomed fluted flan tin.
6. Use the rolling pin to pick the pastry up and lay it over the tin. Gently press the pastry into the tin so that it fills all the contours. Be careful not to stretch the pastry or it will tear, or shrink back in the oven. Return it to the fridge for another 30 minutes, or more if the pastry still feels soft. Reserve the scraps.

Almond Filling

1. Place the butter in a mixing bowl and soften in the microwave on a low heat.
2. Attach a beater, add the sugar, ground almonds and golden syrup and blend lightly together. Do not cream the mixture.
3. Slowly add the warmed eggs. Scrape down the sides of the bowl.
4. Add the flour and almond essence. Blend all ingredients together until well combined. Do not overmix.
5. Fill the tart base with the almond filling.
6. Place directly into a preheated oven set at 190°C. Bake for 18–20 minutes. Be careful not to overbake.
7. Once cool remove from the flan tin.
8. Spread the topping (see recipe below) on the cold almond tart.
9. Grill the top to a golden brown colour under a low heat. Be careful not to burn the top.

Honey and Almond Topping

1. Place all ingredients in a heavy bottomed saucepan.
2. Bring to the boil, stirring gently for 1 minute.
3. Use immediately.

DEAN BRETTSCHNEIDER

Dean (author of this baking book) is a committed baker who travels extensively around New Zealand for Goodman Fielder Milling and Baking to advise professional bakers. His expertise is well respected, and he is seen as an innovative and skilled craftsman with a penchant for troubleshooting in the bakery.

He owned his own bakery and takes pleasure in 'messing about' in the kitchen at home, developing innovative baking recipes and perfecting the classics. Here he shares three such recipes.

Cracked Pepper and Parmesan Crackers

These crackers are thick and crunchy, and ideal for serving with your favourite pâté, dip or cheese. Store in an airtight container or wrap in cellophane bags and tie with a ribbon for a special gift.

1. Place all the ingredients except the water onto a work surface. Make a well and add the water.
2. Mix or knead the dough by hand using the technique shown in the All About Bread section. Continue kneading until the ingredients are well combined. This final kneading should take about 10–15 minutes (check if you have fully developed the dough by using the stretch test).
3. Place the dough in a lightly oiled bowl, cover with plastic and leave in a warmish place (23–25°C) for 30 minutes.
4. Gently knock back the dough in the bowl. This will deflate it slightly, but will develop more strength. Cover again and leave for 20 minutes.
5. Tip the dough out onto a lightly floured bench. Flatten and roll the dough out to a rectangle 30 cm x 42 cm and 3 mm in thickness.
6. Roll the dough up on the rolling pin and unroll onto a baking tray lined with baking paper. Ensure the rectangle is still the same size as in step 5.
7. Using a fork, prick the dough all over (the more holes the better).
8. Lightly spray or brush the surface with water and sprinkle with parmesan cheese or sesame seeds.
9. Using a large chef's knife cut the dough into even rectangles, each one 7 cm x 4 cm.
10. Cover with a proofing cloth or clean tea towel and leave in a warm, draught-free place to prove for 45 minutes.
11. Place directly into a preheated oven set at 180°C and bake for 30 minutes.
12. Lower the oven temperature to 160°C and bake for a further 10 minutes with the oven door ajar.
13. Remove from the oven and using a sharp knife cut down the cut marks that were made before proofing and baking. This must be done as soon as the crackers come out of the oven.
14. Once cut place onto a cooling wire.

250 g Champion or Elfin High Grade Flour
5 g gluten flour
5 g salt
8 g Elfin Dried Yeast (1 sachet)
55 g butter or baking margarine
5 g cracked pepper
20 g kibbled wheat
20 g kibble rye
20 g rolled oats
20 g linseed
20 g pearl barley
20 g sesame seeds
20 g coarsely ground corn grits or polenta
15 g parmesan cheese
180 ml water (25°C)

Ciabatta

Ciabatta is a favourite bread from Italy that has taken the world by storm and turns up in many innovative bakeries. It is a very complex bread to bake, requiring a lot of skill and knowledge. It has a golden brown crust and the moist interior has large airy holes. Dean has perfected the technique but warns that this bread should not be attempted by novice bakers.

STARTER

200 g Champion or Elfin High Grade Flour

$\frac{1}{4}$ teaspoon Elfin Dried Yeast

100 ml water (25°C)

DOUGH

500 g Champion or Elfin High Grade Flour

10 g gluten flour

5 g Elfin Dried Yeast

300 g biga starter

450 g water (25°C)

10 g salt

5 g olive oil

semolina or flour for dusting

Biga Starter (make the day before)

1. Place the flour and yeast onto your work surface. Make a well and add the water.
2. Knead the dough for 5 minutes until a very firm dough is formed.
3. Place in a lightly oiled container, cover and leave at room temperature overnight or for 12 hours.

Dough

1. Sieve the flour and gluten onto your work surface. Make a well.
2. Add the yeast, biga starter (cut into 8–10 pieces) and 320 ml of the water to the well.
3. Knead the dough for 5 minutes.
4. Place the dough in a bowl, cover and rest for 15 minutes.
5. Add the salt and olive oil, and continue to knead until the dough is smooth, elastic and fully developed (15 minutes). Use the stretch test to tell when the dough is fully developed. Cover and rest for 5 minutes.
6. Very slowly, gently knead in the balance of the water (130 ml), approximately 1 tablespoon at a time, kneading well before the next addition of water. Avoid adding too much water at once as this will cause the dough to slosh about and make it very difficult to knead. All the water must be added, so the dough will be very wet but when stretched it should still hold together and form a thin membrane. This process should take approximately 15 minutes.
7. Place the dough in a lightly oiled, flat container (to assist in transferring the dough from the bench to the container, dip your hands into water, as this will stop the dough sticking to your hands). Cover and rest for 15 minutes.
8. Gently knock back the dough by folding it inwards to expel the gases. Lightly oil the container again and return the dough, cover again and leave for 1 hour to double in size. Sprinkle your work surface heavily with semolina or flour.
9. Very gently tip or pour the dough out onto the floured bench. Sprinkle the top surface of the dough with semolina or flour.
10. Form a rectangle by gently pressing and stretching the dough until it is 4 cm thick. Avoid too much pressure with your hands as this will cause the dough to deflate and lose all the gases.
11. Leave the dough to rest for a further 5 minutes.
12. While the dough is resting, place a sheet of baking paper onto a clean baking tray. Sprinkle the baking paper heavily with semolina or flour.
13. Using your dough scraper, trim the outside edges and cut the dough into three equal rectangles.
14. Using your hands gently lift the dough pieces and place directly onto the baking

tray dusted with semolina or flour. Ensure there is a 2.5 cm gap between each piece.

15. Lightly sprinkle the top surface of the ciabatta again with semolina or flour. Cover with a proofing cloth or clean tea towel.

16. Place the ciabatta in a warm place for 35 minutes to proof. To test for readiness, lightly press your finger into the dough – it should feel soft and alive, no longer sticky and wet.

17. Preheat your oven to 250°C. With a baking stone or a hot oven tray in your oven, gently slide the ciabatta (which is still on the baking paper) directly onto the baking stone or a hot oven tray.

18. Spray the oven with water to create steam or have a pan filled with water within the oven. Repeat the spraying 2–3 times during the first 5 minutes of baking.

19. Reduce the oven temperature to 230°C and bake for 25 minutes before opening the oven door.

20. Turn the ciabatta in the oven to ensure even baking. Bake for a further 15 minutes with the oven temperature set at 200°C. Ensure that the ciabatta are well baked and a hollow sound is heard when the bottom is tapped. The loaves should be light when picked up.

21. Place onto a wire cooling rack.

Dessert Pizza

Now that pizza appears on menus everywhere, from cafés through to upmarket restaurants, this dessert pizza is bound to be popular with young and old. It is a fun dessert with lots of delicious chocolate and caramel topped off with fresh fruit.

1. Sieve the flour onto your work surface. Make a well and add the salt, sugar and yeast.
2. Slowly add the water and $\frac{3}{4}$ of the egg. Knead the dough for 6–7 minutes or until the dough is almost fully developed (it is important to develop the gluten structure before all the egg is added).
3. Continue to add the balance of the egg slowly while the dough is still being kneaded. Add sufficient egg to achieve a very soft, elastic, smooth and shiny dough.
4. While kneading slowly add the softened butter in small amounts. Knead in all the butter to achieve a smooth, elastic, silky dough. Do not overmix the dough as this will cause overheating and the dough will become oily and greasy.
5. Transfer the dough into a lightly oiled container covered with plastic wrap, and give a bulk fermentation time of 1 hour in a warm, draught-free place. The dough should have doubled in size.
6. Gently knock back the dough to expel all the gases, reactivate the yeast and strengthen the gluten structure. Finally, push the dough out to a thickness of 5 cm, place into a shallow container, and cover with plastic wrap.
7. Place in the refrigerator overnight (12 hours). This makes the dough easier to work and mould since the dough will be cold and firm.
8. The following day scale off into two 250 g pieces. Mould both pieces into a round ball, and rest for 5 minutes in the refrigerator. If you only require one base, wrap the other base in plastic wrap and return to the refrigerator. Use within 2 days.
9. On a lightly floured work surface, roll each dough ball out to a 30 cm circle, 3–4 mm thick.
10. Place onto a baking tray lined with baking paper, ensuring that the circle is round and 3 mm thick.
11. Using 85 g of moulding chocolate (see recipe overleaf) roll out into a 80 cm long rope. Place this rope around the outside edge of the dough, 2 cm in from the edge.
12. Lightly brush or spray the dough with water. Fold the outside dough over the chocolate rope and seal firmly to ensure the chocolate rope is encased in dough (be careful not to break or puncture the dough). Egg wash the rim of the dough.
13. Spread 80 g of crème patisserie (see recipe overleaf) evenly over the base.
14. Place the warm caramel (see recipe overleaf) inside a paper piping bag and drizzle over the crème patisserie, ensuring an even amount is drizzled on.
15. Place the fruit (in order) over the crème patisserie and caramel (you may wish to add your own combination of fruits). Drizzle with melted chocolate after applying all the fruit.

BRIOCHE BASE
250 g Champion or Elfin High Grade Flour
5 g salt
25 g granulated sugar
5 g Elfin Dried Yeast (1 sachet)
25 ml water
165 g eggs ($3\frac{1}{2}$) (variable)
125 g softened butter

Finished dough temperature: 27°C

TOPPING
egg wash to seal
10–15 slices of banana
25 g blueberries (fresh or frozen)
25 g sliced peaches (fresh or frozen)
20 g passionfruit pulp or sliced figs
15 g broken milk chocolate buttons
30 g broken white chocolate buttons
6–8 pecan halves
icing sugar and mint leaves for garnish

vanilla ice-cream to serve

Dough — Moulding Chocolate

16. Place the pizza base in a warm, draught-free place for 25–30 minutes to proof.
17. Place directly into a preheated oven set at 200°C and bake for 12–15 minutes.
18. Remove from the oven and evenly place 30 g of fresh raspberries over the other toppings.
19. Lightly dust with icing sugar.
20. Garnish with fresh mint leaves.
21. Serve hot or cold with vanilla ice cream.

Crème Patisserie

CRÈME
125 ml milk
55 g granulated sugar
25 g egg ($^1/_2$)
35 g Champion or Elfin Standard Plain Flour
20 g butter
10 ml rum, Kahlua or Baileys liqueur

1. Place the milk and half the sugar in a saucepan. Stir and bring to the boil.
2. Meanwhile in a bowl whisk the egg and the remaining sugar until the mixture becomes pale yellow and thick.
3. Slowly add the flour to the egg and sugar mixture while still whisking to avoid any lumps. Do not overmix.
4. Once the milk has come to the boil, add half of this to the sugar/egg and flour batter. Stir constantly with a whisk.
5. Return this mixture to the remaining milk in the saucepan and whisk together to avoid any lumps forming.
6. Place on a low heat and cook the mixture until it thickens, stirring all the time. Increase the heat to bring the mixture to the boil and cook for 3 minutes while still stirring.
7. Remove from the heat and whisk in the butter. Then whisk in the alcohol.
8. Transfer into a bowl and cover with plastic wrap. Cool completely before using. This is important.

Caramel

CARAMEL
100 g condensed milk
20 g butter
15 g golden syrup
10 g soft brown sugar

1. Place all the ingredients in a microwave-proof bowl and stir to combine all the ingredients.
2. Place into the microwave and cook on high for $1^1/_2$ minutes, stirring every 20–30 seconds to avoid overcooking the caramel. This is possible due to the small amount of caramel in the bowl.

Moulding Chocolate

CHOCOLATE
55 g liquid glucose
110 g melted milk chocolate

1. Place the glucose in a small bowl and warm to approximately 30°C.
2. Add the melted chocolate and stir until the two ingredients are well combined (the mixture will appear to be very oily; do not panic at this stage).
3. Wrap the mixture in plastic wrap and leave overnight. The mixture will firm up.
4. Unwrap the moulding chocolate and soften by working it in your hands. Mould or roll as required. Any unused moulding chocolate should be stored in plastic wrap and kept in an airtight container to prevent skinning.

DIXON STREET DELI

*T*hree generations of the Chait family have been involved in the bustling Dixon St Deli in the heart of Wellington. From the 1930s through to the 1970s it was known as the Farm Poultry Supply Company and historic photos displayed around the walls today give a glimpse of the early retailing days.

Jayne, wife of second generation Martin Chait, learnt to bake traditional Jewish breads in a London deli in 1980. She returned to New Zealand and introduced Jewish rye bread, the first bagels in New Zealand, savoury pirogue, and a farmer's bread to the Wellington customers. The demand for these breads saw the business expand to a bakery in Brooklyn 10 years ago and it now supplies around 50 wholesale customers, some as far away as Auckland.

The bakery is now managed by third generation Ari Chait, who declares that 'baking is a very noble trade – in fact, the more I think about it, the more I like it!'

Authentic Bagels

The classic method of making bagels is revealed in this recipe. The interior should be soft and moist and the crust very chewy. As bagels are best eaten the day they're baked, use day-old bagels to make crisps which are excellent with spreads and dips.

1. Sieve the flour onto your work surface. Make a well and add the gluten, salt, sugar, olive oil, yeast and water.
2. Mix or knead the dough by hand using the technique shown in the All About Bread section. Every couple of minutes stop and check the gluten development and temperature of the dough. This final kneading should take about 10–15 minutes (check if you have fully developed the dough by using the stretch test). At this stage the dough should be firm and cool.
3. Using your dough scraper divide the dough into 100 g pieces. You should have 12 dough pieces.
4. Round each dough piece into a tight ball, cover with plastic or a clean tea towel. Give an intermediate proof of 10 minutes.
5. Roll each ball into a 20 cm long sausage shape, ensuring that it is an even thickness from end to end.
6. Wrap the elongated dough piece around your four fingers with the two ends meeting together underneath your fingers. Applying pressure on the bench, roll the ends together to create a seal and ultimately forming the distinctive ring shape (see photograph opposite).
7. Once the bagels are formed place onto a baking tray (or suitable trays that will fit into your refrigerator) dusted with fine corn grits or semolina and place in the refrigerator overnight (maximum of 16 hours). Allow approximately 2 cm space around each bagel.
8. Remove from the refrigerator and stand at room temperature for 45–60 minutes. While the bagels are recovering, put a large saucepan of hot water onto a high heat (with the lid on) and bring to the boil.
9. While the water is boiling, remove the lid and place three bagels at a time into the boiling water. Blanch for 30 seconds on each side, a total of 1 minute.
10. Using a slotted spoon gently remove the bagels, ensuring that all the water has drained off. Place bottom side down onto a greased or baking paper-lined baking tray (allow approximately 2 cm space around each bagel).
11. Toppings can be applied at this stage, for example, sesame seeds, poppy seeds, grated cheese or finely sliced onion, etc.
12. Place a full tray of bagels into a preheated oven set at 200°C. Bake for 20–25 minutes until shiny and golden brown.
13. Place on a cooling rack.

750 g Champion or Elfin High Grade Flour
30 g gluten flour
20 g salt
25 g soft brown sugar
15 g olive oil
10 g Elfin Dried Yeast
430 ml chilled water (placed in the refrigerator overnight)

Finished dough temperature: 25°C

Variations

Onion Bagel
– If using dried onions add an extra 60 ml of water.
– Add 65 g of dried onion flakes (or finely chopped fresh onion) directly to the dough at step 1.
– Process as for standard bagel.

Cinnamon and Raisin Bagel
– Increase the Elfin Dried Yeast to 16 g.
– Increase the water to 60 ml.
– Add 15 g of ground cinnamon directly to the dough after three-quarters of the dough development (near the end of step 2). Knead in well until the cinnamon is evenly dispersed.
– Add 115 g of raisins to the dough once full dough development has been achieved (at the end of step 2). Knead in gently to avoid crushing the raisins.
– Process as for standard bagel.

Chocolate Chip Bagel
– Add 45 g of cocoa powder to the dough at step 1.
– Increase the water to 60 ml.
– Add 115 g of chilled chocolate chips to the dough once full dough development has been achieved (at the end of step 2). Knead in gently.
– Process as for standard bagel.

Bagel Crisps
– Once the bagels are 2–3 days old, using a sharp bread knife, carefully slice the bagel horizontally as thinly as possible to form 3–4 mm thick bagel discs. In a commercial bakery you can use a bacon slicer.
– Place the thinly sliced bagel discs onto a baking tray and toast under the grill set at 150°C until light golden brown; turn over and repeat. These are great served with guacamole or your favourite dip. You can also place them into a cellophane bag tied with a ribbon for that special gift.

Caraway Rye Bread

Jane Chait learnt this classic Jewish bread recipe while working in London and introduced it to Dixon St Deli customers in the early 80s. It is enormously popular and full of flavour. The process of making this bread involves making the 'sour' over three days before actually mixing the dough.

To make the sour

DAY 1

1. Mix all the ingredients together in a clean bowl.
2. Using a wooden spoon stir until combined, then scrape down the sides of the bowl.
3. Cover with muslin cloth and place in a warm place to ferment until the next day (maximum of 18 hours).

DAY 2

Mix ingredients as for Day 1.

DAY 3

Mix ingredients as for Day 1.

DAY 4

1. Sieve the two flours onto your work surface. Make a well and add the rye sour, salt, caraway seeds, yeast and water.
2. Mix or knead the dough by hand using the technique shown in the All About Bread section. Continue to knead the dough by hand. Every couple of minutes stop and check the gluten development and temperature of the dough. This final kneading should take about 10–15 minutes (check if you have fully developed the dough by using the stretch test).
3. Lightly oil a bowl large enough to allow the dough to double in bulk. Put the dough in the bowl and cover with plastic. Leave in a warmish place (23–25°C) and give a bulk fermentation time of 30 minutes.
4. Gently knock back the dough, cover with plastic again and leave for a further 15 minutes.
5. Tip the dough out onto the bench which has been lightly dusted with flour.
6. Using a dough scraper, divide the dough in half.
7. Gently shape each dough piece into a ball or cob shape.
8. Place on a lightly floured bench and give an intermediate proof of 10 minutes, covered with plastic. While you wait, lightly dust a proofing cloth or tea towel with rye flour.
9. Uncover the dough and remould into a smooth tight vienna shape. The surface of the dough should be stretched tightly over the mass, and there should be a neat seam along one side. Lay the first loaf on the proofing cloth, but before laying the second loaf down pleat the cloth so that the loaves cannot touch as they rise.
10. Final proof for approximately 45–55 minutes in a warm, draught-free place. Cover with plastic to prevent skinning and chilling of the dough. Use the

DAY 1

40 g rye flour (not ryemeal)

40 ml water at 28°C

$^1/_4$ tablespoon Elfin Dry Yeast (from a sachet of yeast; keep in the refrigerator until day 4)

DAY 2

81 g sour (from above)

80 g rye flour

80 ml water at 32°C

DAY 3

241 g sour (from above)

240 g rye flour

120 ml water at 32°C

DAY 4

100 g rye flour

700 g Champion or Elfin High Grade Flour

601 g sour (from above)

20 g salt

25 g caraway seeds

7 g Elfin Dry Yeast (balance of sachet from day 1)

460 ml water

Final dough temperature: 28°C

indentation test to tell when the dough is three-quarter proofed. These loaves are dense in texture so you will not achieve the same volume as a white loaf.

11. The oven should be preheated to 220°C, with a baking stone in place. Gently tip one loaf out onto a peel lightly dusted with semolina.

12. Dust the loaves lightly with rye flour.

13. Using a razor blade or sharp knife, make four diagonal cuts in the top of the loaves.

14. Just before you load the bread into the oven, spray water into the oven cavity. Close the door quickly so you don't lose any of the steam.

15. With the peel and loaf in one hand, open the oven door with the other, and gently 'flick' the loaf off the peel and onto the baking stone. Close the oven door immediately.

16. Repeat this for the second loaf, but be careful not to spray water directly onto the first loaf. Close the door again and wait 2 minutes before opening the door slightly and spraying more water into the oven. Two minutes later, 'steam' the oven again. Resist opening the door for another 20 minutes.

17. Turn the heat down to 200°C, and check the loaves for even baking. If necessary, turn them around. For the remaining time leave the door of the oven slightly ajar to thicken and dry the crust.

18. After a total of 30–40 minutes the loaves will be ready. Cool on a wire rack.

ROLAND DALLAS

DOVEDALE FOODS

Deep in the valley beyond Moutere, about 50 kilometres from Nelson, the Dovedale bakery hides in an old tobacco kiln set amongst leafy trees and surrounded by paddocks, views of the distant hills and absolute peace. Roland Dallas, his wife Christine and their two daughters sought a quieter, calmer lifestyle after running a busy Christchurch bakery, Dallas Bread, and now bake on three days a week for numerous retail outlets and private customers throughout New Zealand.

Roland is totally committed to baking bread with wholesome organic ingredients, and produces a mere five product lines including a popular rice bread which is the mainstay of the business. This is free of yeasts, gluten and wheat flour so it finds favour throughout the country with those on special diets. Uncompromising in standards, with the best organic flours and grains sourced from Australia, Roland has perfected the art of natural yeasts for fermentation. (See following notes for his philosophy on this.)

A creative baker, ably assisted by Paula Williamson (below), he does occasionally produce pastries and Italian-style rustic breads for special local events. His fruity buns and a smooth Scottish bannock, available year round, are supplemented at Christmas and Easter with a fruity stollen. His business is more than passion for baking: it is about a lifestyle and a niche market that work remarkably well.

A Note on Ingredients and Leavens

We at Dovedale Foods use only organic stoneground flours and grains in our breads. We recommend their use in leaven breads. The power of a leaven ferment can be affected by many factors, including chemicals in over-refined flours, pesticide residues in conventional flour and chlorine in water.

In addition, stoneground flours are ground at lower temperatures, ensuring that nutritional properties are left intact, thus providing more food for the leaven to feed on.

It is important to understand the difference between the wild yeasts of leaven fermentation and the commercial baker's yeast used in most breads. There are over 400 different species of yeast microfungi. Baker's yeast is one single species (Saccharomyces cerevisiae), a purified virulent strain bred for fast, uniform development.

Leavens or sourdoughs, however, are usually leavened by multiple wild yeast species of lower virulence, and less uniform characteristics. True leaven or sourdough breads are the product of not only wild yeasts but also beneficial bacteria called lactobacilli, which produce lactic acid and contribute to the piquant flavour.

The longevity of the people of the Caucasus Mountains has been attributed to their high intake of lactobacilli and acidophillus, through the consumption of yoghurt and traditionally fermented bread.

Lactobacilli require at least eight hours to develop in a leaven. Since the introduction of commercial baker's yeast last century, shorter proving times have meant that lactobacilli have been missing from the modern loaf.

Lactobacilli and wild yeasts are in the air all around us. They are diverse in their composition, reflecting differences in flavour from area to area.

Here in Dovedale we enjoy a rural environment with close proximity to beech and pine forests and hedgerows of hawthorn and barberry. Just as the juniper bushes of the Yukon and the sourdoughs of San Francisco give a distinct flavour to those regions' traditional breads, so too does our Dovedale environment dictate the flavour of our ferments.

Dovedale Rye and Linseed

With the nutty crunch of the linseed and the full flavour of rye, this is a bread that you will want to cook often. It is quite moist and will keep well for a few days. Try it toasted when the flavour really comes out well.

1. Mix all ingredients in a bowl, then knead on the bench for 10–15 minutes. The dough will be sticky in texture, similar to that of a stiff biscuit dough. You will not achieve a smooth elastic developed dough as rye flour does not contain any elastic and extensible gluten-forming proteins.
2. Using your dough scraper divide the dough into three pieces at 800 g each.
3. On a lightly floured bench, shape the dough into a oblong roll.
4. Place into greased bread tins, ensuring the smooth side is at the top and the seam is at the bottom.
5. Cover the tins with plastic and proof in a warm place for 3–4 hours. Correct proof has been achieved when the dough has small bubbles and holes on the dough's surface and when the dough has risen approximately 3.5 cm from its original height. This indicates that maximum gassing has been achieved.
6. Place the proved loaves directly into a preheated oven set at 215°C. Bake the tins on the oven stone to achieve a solid bake.
7. Bake for 1 hour, or until the hollow sound is heard when the bottom is tapped.
8. Place on a cooling rack.

80 g linseed (soaked for 12 hours in 120 ml of boiling water)
1 kg organic rye flour
15 g sea salt
600 g rye leaven (see making a leaven, using only rye flour)
600 ml water (25°C)

Making a Dovedale Leaven

A leaven is a mixture of flour and water of porridge-like consistency. Two parts flour to three parts water should make a wet mix with the pouring qualities of a batter.

STAGE 1

200 g organic white flour (or this can be replaced with any organic flour)

200 g filtered water (25°C)

STAGE 2

600 g organic flour

900 g filtered water (25°C)

STAGE 1

Mix the initial starter in an earthenware or stainless steel bowl; cover with a tea towel and leave for a minimum of 48 hours at room temperature.

At this point, the flour and water should have separated. It will have a slightly sour odour with a few bubbles on the surface and the flour will be discoloured.

STAGE 2

Add more flour and water to the starter, this time with three times the amount of flour and water used in the initial starter.

Cover again and leave at least 8 hours.

STAGE 3

The leaven will now be at optimum gassing power with a thick, foaming consistency bubbling with life and a distinct beer-like sour aroma. This is the time to harness the wild yeast activity and make your final dough.

Dovedale Gluten-Free Rice-Millet Bread

The perfect answer for people who have allergies to mainstream breads, this is Dovedale's most popular selling line. It contains no wheat, gluten or yeast and the resulting loaf is moist and dense.

300 g millet

1 lt water (25°C)

1 kg organic brown rice flour

20 g sea salt

60 g maize starch

1 lt rice flour leaven (see making a leaven, using only rice flour)

1. Bring the millet and 660 ml of the water to the boil and simmer for 20 minutes. Cool before use.
2. Mix all ingredients in a mixing bowl, including the balance of the water, then knead on the bench for 10–15 minutes. The dough will be sticky in texture, similar to that of a stiff biscuit dough. You will not achieve a smooth elastic developed dough as rice flour does not contain any elastic and extensible gluten-forming proteins.
3. Using your dough scraper, divide the dough into five pieces at 800g each.
4. On a lightly floured bench, shape the dough into an oblong roll.
5. Place into greased bread tins, ensuring the smooth side is at the top and the seam is at the bottom.
6. Cover the tins with plastic and proof in a warm place for 3–4 hours. Correct proof has been achieved when the dough has small bubbles and holes on the dough's surface, and when the dough has risen approximately 3.5 cm from its original height. This indicates that maximum gassing has been achieved.
7. Place the proved loaves directly into a preheated oven set at 200°C. Bake the tins on the oven stone to achieve a solid bake.
8. Bake for $1\frac{1}{2}$–2 hours, or until a hollow sound is heard when the bottom is tapped.
9. Place on a cooling rack.

HEAVENS' BAKERY

One of the cornerstones of New Zealand's baking industry, Graham Heaven (right) is remarkably enthusiastic about baking after 22 years of working through the night to have bread ready for his customers each morning. Three times Baker of the Year, Graham's business involves running five retail outlets in the Napier region, and he has trained 26 apprentices, some of whom are still working for him.

His whole life revolves around baking: his family, including son Jason, are immersed in the business, his best friends are bakers, and he is on the executive of the New Zealand Baking Society. Innovative ideas are sought on his frequent overseas trips (although the bestselling line in Napier remains the white loaf), and Graham opened one of the country's very first hot bread shops, a concept that is still wildly popular today. His philosophy is to push new products with tastings and promotions, and he has seen his perseverance pay off as his customers adopt the influences from European baking that are shaping the industry's future.

Deluxe Shortbread

Shortbread is great to have on hand for it is perennially popular with young and old. The texture is meltingly smooth.

1. Sieve the icing sugar into a mixing bowl. Add the softened butter and, using the beater attachment, cream until light and fluffy.
2. Sieve the flour, custard powder and salt together.
3. Mix the sieved dry ingredients into the creamed mixture. Mix well until the mixture comes together in one lump.
4. Lightly flour your work surface and roll out until 1.5 cm thick. Cut into desired shapes.
5. Place on a baking paper lined baking tray, spread apart slightly. Prick with a fork.
6. Bake in a preheated oven set at 150°C for 30 minutes or until very pale gold in colour.
7. Remove from the oven and immediately dredge with caster sugar if desired.

Note: this recipe is also suited to the following:

340 g softened butter
170 g icing sugar
*385 g Champion or Elfin Standard
 Plain Flour*
125 g Edmonds Custard Powder
good pinch of salt
caster sugar for dredging

Pressed or Moulded Shortbread

1. Make shortbread as for standard recipe (steps 1 to 3).
2. Using a round cutter, cut rolled shortbread into circles.
3. Lightly dust your shortbread press or mould with flour. Firmly press the mould into the surface of the shortbread.
4. Gently place on a baking paper lined baking tray.
5. Bake as for standard shortbread.

Refrigerated Shortbread

1. Make shortbread as for standard recipe (steps 1 to 3).
2. Roll shortbread into thick sausage shape logs, approximately 5 cm in diameter.
3. Wrap the log in plastic wrap and place in the refrigerator for 2–3 hours until firm all the way through.
4. Remove from the refrigerator and take off the plastic wrap. Using a sharp cook's knife carefully slice off discs of shortbread 1.5 cm thick. The shortbread dough can also be frozen at this point by wrapping in plastic wrap.
5. Place the shortbread discs flat on a baking paper lined baking tray.
6. Bake as for standard shortbread.

Honey Roll

With spicy notes and a strong honey flavour, this rolled cake is perfect for dessert or for serving with coffee. Take care with the mixture as it is fairly liquid before baking.

CAKE

150 g golden syrup

150 g honey (creamed type)

65 g softened butter

75 g eggs (1$^1/_2$)

65 ml milk (warm)

5 g baking soda

165 g Champion or Elfin Standard
   Plain Flour

5 g ground ginger

5 g ground cinnamon

coconut for rolling

CREAM

200 g softened butter

50 ml cold water

15 g cornflour

15 g milk powder

150 ml boiling water

200 g icing sugar

3 drops vanilla essence

1. Place golden syrup, honey and softened butter in a mixing bowl, and using a beater, beat together until light in colour. Scrape down the mixing bowl.
2. Add the egg, mixing to combine on a low speed for 1–2 minutes.
3. Warm the milk and stir in the soda. Add directly to the egg mixture.
4. Take off mixer and fold in sieved dry ingredients by hand. Mix by hand until clear. Don't overmix.
5. Pour the mixture (which is in a liquid form, and not as firm as a sponge) into 20 x 30 cm or larger sponge roll tin, greased and lined with greaseproof paper. Spread level.
6. Bake immediately at 180°C for 20–30 minutes.
7. Cool slightly and turn out onto a sheet of greaseproof paper finely sprinkled with coconut (top surface of baked honey roll on the coconut). Cool completely.
8. Spread a thin layer of butter cream over as for swiss roll (see recipe below).
9. Roll up as for swiss roll from the short edge (coconut prevents top surface from sticking to the paper).
10. Roll up tightly in greaseproof paper, do not unroll for 1 hour (this prevents the roll from unrolling or cracking).
11. Unroll and trim edges.
12. Cut into slices and serve.

Butter Cream

1. Place the softened butter in a mixing bowl and, using a beater, cream until light and fluffy.
2. Make a slurry out of the cold water, cornflour and milk powder.
3. Place the boiling water in a saucepan on a medium heat and add the slurry. Cook through until the mixture thickens and forms a custard, stirring to prevent burning. Cool slightly.
4. Sieve the icing sugar and stir into the warm custard. Cool completely.
5. Add the icing sugar/custard mix to the creamed, fluffy butter and beat until a light butter cream is formed.

Note: unused butter cream can be stored in the refrigerator in an airtight container until required. Simply warm to soften, and beat until light and fluffy.

ALISON WESTOBY

HILLYERS OF LINCOLN

*F*or almost 30 years, Hillyers have made a selection of classic New Zealand pies in the tiny town of Lincoln on the outskirts of Christchurch. Alison Westoby (centre) grew up nearby, and after an early career as a school teacher, purchased the business from the Hillyer family as she had always been 'interested in good food' and had a desire to own such a business.

Hillyers' pies are almost legendary in the Canterbury region, and have been available for many years at the respected department store, Ballantynes. Alison has been fortunate enough to retain some of the family staff, and with a sound business advisor is expanding and developing the bakery.

These are pies made with the very best ingredients and there is no compromise on quality or pricing. The customers really appreciate the handmade savoury pies, fruit pies, petits fours, cakes and biscuits, and are prepared to pay a little extra to enjoy this fine fare.

Steak, Caramelised Onion and Red Pepper Mustard Pie

This is a real winner with its tasty steak and rich onion filling. Serve with a green salad for a warming winter lunch. You may wish to purchase puff pastry from the supermarket; however, if you prefer to make your own, follow the recipe below.

Puff Pastry

It is best if the pastry is made one day in advance.

1. Choose the method of making puff pastry from the All About Pastries section.
2. Once you have incorporated the layering fat give the pastry either four 'half folds' or three 'book folds' (see the All About Pastries section).
3. Remove from the refrigerator and roll out to the required thickness and shape stated below.

Filling

1. Place the butter in a saucepan and melt.
2. Add the flour to the butter, and blend until a firm ball of dough is formed and the saucepan is clean.
3. Slowly add a little of the milk and mix in thoroughly. Keep adding small quantities of milk, mixing in each addition thoroughly to prevent lumps.
4. Once all the milk is added to make a runny sauce or roux, add the mustard powder, cracked pepper and salt. Blend in and leave until required.
5. Cut beef into cubes and cook in a saucepan in its own juices.
6. Once the meat is cooked, add enough flour to soak up all the meat juices.
7. Heat the sauce on a moderate heat, stirring constantly until it reaches a thickish consistency.
8. Add the Provençal mustard, crushed garlic and red pepper. Mix until all the ingredients are blended together.
9. Add some of the thick sauce to the meat, stir in, and mix the remainder of the sauce into the meat. Allow to cool.
10. Line the pie dish with puff pastry rolled out to 3–4 mm thick. (See pastry recipe above.)
11. Place the beef sauce mix into each pie base and fill to three-quarters.
12. Add a layer of caramelised onion slices (see recipe below).
13. Make the puff pastry lids from the rolled pastry. Wash the edge of the pastry bases with water and place the pastry lid on top, seal edges and trim away excess pastry with a sharp knife.
14. Egg wash the top surface. Rest for 1 hour (or longer) before baking.
15. Place directly into a preheated oven set at 220°C and bake for 25 minutes.
16. Allow to cool in the tin for 30 minutes then remove and place on a cooling rack.

Caramelised Onion

1. Slice the onion using a sharp knife.
2. Melt the butter in a frypan and add the sugar.
3. On a high heat add the onion to the butter and sugar mixture. Allow the onion to soften and turn a light golden colour, stirring occasionally.
4. Remove from the heat and cool.

PASTRY
500 g Champion or Elfin High Grade Flour
80 g butter (chilled)
pinch of salt
260 ml water (chilled – place in the refrigerator overnight)
300 g butter (chilled) for layering

FILLING
50 g butter
80 g Champion or Elfin Plain Flour
300 g milk
7 g mustard powder
1 teaspoon cracked pepper
$\frac{1}{2}$ teaspoon salt
350 g beef
80 g Moille Provençal mustard with red pepper and garlic
5 g crushed garlic
120 g chopped red pepper
egg wash to finish

CARAMELISED ONION
1 medium onion, sliced
15 g butter
10 g soft brown sugar

Chicken, Cranberry and Brie Pie

This is a delicious modern filling, which brings a whole new dimension to the classic New Zealand pie. This is a real favourite with the regular customers at Hillyers. You may wish to purchase puff pastry from the supermarket, or follow the recipe below.

Puff Pastry

It is best if the pastry is made one day in advance.

1. Choose the method of making puff pastry from the All About Pastries section.
2. Once you have incorporated the layering fat give the pastry either four 'half folds' or three 'book folds' (see the All About Pastries section).
3. Remove from the refrigerator and roll out to the required thickness and shape stated below.

Filling

1. Place the butter in a saucepan and melt over a medium heat.
2. Add the flour to the butter. Using a wooden spoon, blend the mixture until a firm ball of dough is formed and the saucepan is clean.
3. Slowly add a little of the milk and mix in thoroughly. Keep adding small quantities of milk, mixing in each addition thoroughly to prevent lumps.
4. Once all the milk is added to make a runny sauce or roux, add the mustard powder, cracked pepper, salt and mixed herbs. Blend in and leave until required.
5. Dice the chicken breast and cook in a saucepan with the garlic. The chicken should cook in its own juices.
6. Once the chicken is cooked, drain the excess juices and add the chicken meat to the sauce. Allow to cool.
7. Line the pie dishes with puff pastry rolled out to 3–4 mm thick.
8. Fill three-quarters of the pie with the chicken filling.
9. Add a circle of cranberry sauce in the centre area on top of the chicken.
10. Place a slice of brie on top of the cranberry sauce.
11. Make the pastry lids from the rolled pastry. Wash the edge of the pastry bases with water and place the lid on top. Seal edges and trim excess pastry off with a sharp knife.
12. Egg wash top surface. Rest for 1 hour (or longer) before baking.
13. Place directly into a preheated oven set at 220°C and bake for 25–30 minutes.
14. Allow to cool in the tins for 30 minutes, then remove and place on a cooling rack.

Photo on previous page

PASTRY

500 g Champion or Elfin High Grade Flour

80 g butter (chilled)

pinch of salt

260 ml water (chilled – place in the refrigerator overnight)

300 g butter (chilled) for layering

FILLING

50 g butter

80 g Champion or Elfin Plain Flour

300 ml milk

17 g mustard powder

1 teaspoon cracked pepper

$\frac{1}{2}$ teaspoon salt

1 teaspoon mixed herbs

300 g chicken breast (diced)

5 g crushed garlic

brie cheese

cranberry sauce

egg wash to finish

Caramel Petits Fours

A real sweet treat amongst the selection of petits fours that Hillyers produces. Perfect for serving with coffee, or wrap four to six individual tarts in cellophane bags, tie with gold or silver ribbon, and give as a special gift.

Sweet Pastry Cases

1. Lightly cream the butter and sugar in a mixing bowl fitted with a beater or in a bowl and beat with a wooden spoon.
2. Add the egg and mix until combined.
3. Lastly add the flour and mix to a paste. Only mix until the paste comes clean off the bowl. Be careful not to overmix or the pastry will become too elastic and doughy.
4. Transfer to a bowl. Cover and refrigerate for 30 minutes or overnight.
5. On a lightly floured workbench roll the pastry out into a sheet about 3 mm thick.
6. Using a 60–65 mm plain round cutter, cut out 24 bases and line mini muffin tins. Ensure that you gently press the pastry inside the tins to avoid any cracking around the bases.

Caramel Filling

1. Place all ingredients in a stainless steel bowl. Stir together with a wooden spoon.
2. Place a saucepan half-filled with water on a moderate heat.
3. Place the bowl full of ingredients into the warming water, stirring constantly to avoid burning the bottom.
4. Heat until a thickish caramel consistency is achieved. Remove from the heat.
5. Spoon the caramel three-quarters of the way up the shortcrust lined tins, top with chocolate chips, neatly placed, then place a walnut half on top.
6. Place in a preheated oven set at 180°C for approximately 15 minutes or until golden brown.
7. Allow to cool slightly, remove from the tins and store in an airtight container.

PASTRY

170 g salted butter

85 g sugar

50 g egg (1)

260 g Champion or Elfin Standard Plain Flour

FILLING

400 g condensed milk

85 g butter

60 g golden syrup

40 g soft brown sugar

1–2 drops vanilla essence

chocolate chips and walnut halves to finish

JANUS BAKKERIJ

Astute customers walking into this city bakery in Wellington's Lambton Quay can almost sense that owner Joseph Janus has baking in his blood. He grew up in Holland and then New Zealand with a grandfather, father and stepfather who were all passionate about their craft, and he is as committed to baking as a baker could be. His training saw him bake in Wainui, Sydney, and a small patisserie, the Mozart, in Amsterdam. His bakery takes infinite care to bake, present and sell bread, cakes and biscuits of the highest standard.

Joseph is quite the perfectionist, very particular about using the best ingredients and detailing his goods so that each is a work of art. There is a constant stream of customers, eating and drinking coffee, or passing through his first floor bakery to purchase lunch on the run or order specialty cakes to take home.

Joseph has observed that his customers' tastes change subtly from the sweet to the savoury as they travel overseas and become more educated about baking. He travels himself to expand his baking repertoire, believing that research and development are crucial to a successful bakery. He works long hours six days a week and is very committed to training his staff to the highest standard. He has trained 15 bakers, and it is full credit to him that they almost all still ply their craft in various places around the country, with the standards of excellence that he has passed on.

Black Forest Gateau

A classic from Europe, the Black Forest gateau is an all-time favourite at the Bakkerij. The cake is dark and moist and, when filled with freshly whipped cream, sticky cherries, a hint of liqueur, and covered in rich chocolate, it is about as sinful and as delicious as a cake could be.

1. Place the egg yolks and sugar in a mixing bowl fitted with a whisk, and whisk until thick and creamy and the mixture has reached the ribbon stage (see section on All About Cakes, Sponges and Biscuits).
2. In a separate, clean, grease-free bowl whisk the egg whites until fluffy and holding a 'stiff peak'.
3. In three additions gently fold the egg whites into the egg yolk and sugar mixture.
4. Sieve the flour and cocoa and fold in until half mixed through.
5. Add the melted butter and melted chocolate, gently fold and combine the ingredients until evenly distributed. Do not overmix at this stage as this will cause the air bubbles to escape and result in a low volume cake base.
6. Gently pour the mixture into a greased 23 cm round cake tin.
7. Place directly into a preheated oven set at 180°C and bake for 40 minutes or until the cake springs back when lightly pressed in the centre.
8. Allow the cake to cool for 15 minutes before removing from the tin.
9. Cool completely then slice the cake horizontally into three even layers.
10. Place the top layer of the cake upside down on the bench so that it becomes the bottom or base of the gateau.
11. Using a pastry brush lightly brush the cake base with kirsch.
12. Using a palette knife spread a thin layer (approximately 5 mm thick) of whipped cream onto the base. Evenly place the cherries all over the cream.
13. Place the middle layer of the cake on top of the whipped cream and cherries, and press down lightly.
14. Repeat steps 11 and 12.
15. Place the last layer of cake on top of the whipped cream and cherries. Ensure the smooth side is on top and the cut side is inside the gateau (see diagram).
16. Holding the palette knife vertically, coat the sides of the gateau with whipped cream, ensuring that there is an even coating all around.
17. Again using the palette knife, spread a layer of whipped cream on the top surface of the gateau, ensuring that you have an even coating. To achieve a smooth and clean finish on the top of the gateau, dip the palette knife into hot water and give the surface one last even spread.
18. Make sure the whipped cream finish is as clean as possible (do not spend too much time re-spreading the top surface as this sometimes causes the cream to be overworked).
19. Place the grated or shaved chocolate onto a sheet of greaseproof paper. Lift up the gateau by sliding the palette knife underneath and tilting it so you can slide the gateau onto the palm of your hand.
20. Use the other hand to scoop up the grated or shaved chocolate, and at the same

CAKE BASE
6 only eggs (separate)
175 g caster sugar
125 g Champion or Elfin Self Rising Flour
25 g cocoa powder
90 g melted butter
150 g melted chocolate

FILLING AND COATING
150 ml kirsch
600 ml fresh cream (whipped and lightly sweetened with sugar)
300 g morello cherries (drained)

DECORATION
grated or shaved chocolate
12 maraschino cherries (with stems on)

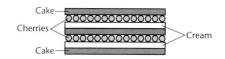

time tilt the gateau (be careful) so that the side of the gateau meets the handful of chocolate. Gently and carefully coat the side of the gateau with chocolate all the way around.

21. Gently and carefully place the gateau onto a serving plate by using a palette knife to ease the gateau off your hand and onto the plate.

22. Fill a piping bag (fitted with a star piping tube) with whipped cream and pipe 12 rosettes around the outside of the gateau.

23. Place a maraschino cherry on each rosette or on every second one.

24. Using a tablespoon, sprinkle grated or shaved chocolate in the middle of the gateau in the shape of a 8 cm circle.

25. Place in the refrigerator to chill before serving.

Note: when cutting a slice of gateau always dip your knife in hot water before cutting.

Chocolate Hazelnut Pretzels

These unusual biscuits are bound to appeal to all chocolate lovers, as they have a luscious chocolate coating which hides a superb soft hazelnut ganache on a crisp chocolate biscuit base. Perfect for a special gift or for serving with coffee.

Chocolate Biscuit Base

1. Lightly cream the butter, salt and sugar in a mixing bowl fitted with a beater, or beat in a bowl with a wooden spoon.
2. Add the egg and mix through.
3. Sieve the flour and cocoa powder and add to the butter and sugar mixture. Only mix until the paste comes clean off the bowl. Be careful not to overmix or the pastry will become too elastic and doughy.
4. Transfer to a bowl. Cover and refrigerate for 30 minutes or overnight.
5. On a lightly floured workbench roll the pastry out into a rectangular sheet about 3 mm thick and 270 mm in length. Cut into strips lengthwise; each strip should be 10 mm wide (see diagram 1).
6. Shape each strip into a pretzel (see diagram 2).
7. Place onto a greased or baking paper lined baking tray.
8. Place directly into a preheated oven set at 175°C and bake for 10–15 minutes or until firm to touch. Cool completely on the baking tray.
9. Using a piping bag fitted with a small plain piping tube, fill with hazelnut ganache (see recipe below). Pipe a ring of filling on top following the shape of the baked pretzel biscuit base. Refrigerate for 10 minutes to firm the filling.
10. Transfer the pretzel bases onto a wire cooling rack and place directly over a sheet of greaseproof paper.
11. Using a ladle, pour thinned melted dark chocolate over each pretzel (see the Ingredients section on how to melt chocolate), ensuring that the pretzel is fully coated with chocolate (except underneath the bases, of course). Tap the cooling wire a few times to remove the excess chocolate.
12. Before the chocolate has set, carefully place each pretzel onto a clean sheet of greaseproof paper.
13. Make a small paper piping bag and fill it with melted white chocolate. Snip off the end to make a fine point and drizzle the chocolate over, resulting in fine white chocolate lines over the pretzel.

Hazelnut Ganache Filling

1. Place the cream and instant coffee in a saucepan and bring to the boil. Remove from the heat.
2. Add the white chocolate and stir with a wooden spoon until the chocolate has completely melted.
3. Transfer to a mixing bowl and whisk the mixture until the ganache has become white and fluffy (like butter cream).
4. While still whisking, add the ground hazelnuts and whisk until well combined.
5. Place into a piping bag and use as directed above.

Note: when piping ganache you must use while still soft and fluffy. If the mixture sits too long it will firm up and become difficult to pipe. If this is the case simply put back into the mixing bowl and whisk until soft and fluffy again.

BISCUIT BASE
135 g butter
pinch of salt
65 g icing sugar
25 g egg ($^1/_2$)
200 g Champion or Elfin Standard Plain Flour
5 g cocoa powder

COATING AND DECORATION
melted dark chocolate
melted white chocolate

FILLING
100 g fresh cream
2 teaspoons instant coffee
225 g white chocolate buttons
50 g ground hazelnuts

1

2

Dutch Apricot Flan

This delicious flan is one of many superb treats from the Janus Bakkerij. With its three components – a sweet pastry base, a moist, fruity apricot layer and a meltingly sweet piped top dusted with icing sugar – this is well worth the effort, and is a great accompaniment to coffee or tea.

FILLING

200 g dried apricots

120 ml hot water

30 g granulated sugar

120 ml hot water

40 ml cold water

10 g cornflour

40 g granulated sugar

$\frac{1}{4}$ teaspoon citric acid

PASTRY

170 g salted butter

85 g sugar

50 g egg (1)

260 g Champion or Elfin Standard
    Plain Flour

TOPPING

40 g icing sugar

125 g softened butter

1–2 drops vanilla essence

125 g Champion or Elfin Standard
    Plain Flour

15 g cornflour

Apricot Filling

1. Place the dried apricots and 120 ml of hot water in a saucepan, bring to the boil and cook for 5 minutes on a medium heat. Tip into a bowl.
2. In the same saucepan bring the 30 g of sugar and the other 120 ml of hot water to the boil.
3. Make a slurry with the cold water and cornflour and then add to the hot sugar and water solution and cook through on a medium heat until it thickens and forms a gel. Remove from the heat and stir in the last amount of sugar until dissolved.
4. Add the apricots and citric acid, place into a food processor or mincer and blend or mince together until well combined.
5. Place in a bowl and cool before using.

Note: this filling can be kept in the refrigerator in a covered bowl for up to 3 days.

Sweet Pastry Base

1. Lightly cream the butter and sugar in a mixing bowl fitted with a beater, or beat in a bowl with a wooden spoon.
2. Add the egg and mix until combined.
3. Add the flour and mix to a paste. Only mix until the paste comes clean off the bowl. Be careful not to overmix or the pastry will become too elastic and doughy.
4. Transfer to a bowl. Cover and refrigerate for 30 minutes or overnight.
5. On a lightly floured workbench roll the pastry out into a sheet about 5 mm thick, and big enough to cover a 20 cm greased fluted loose bottomed tin.
6. Use the rolling pin to pick the pastry up and lay it over the tin. Gently press the pastry into the tin so that it fills all the contours. Be careful not to stretch the pastry or it will tear, or shrink back in the oven. Return it to the fridge for another 30 minutes, or more if the pastry still feels soft. Reserve the scraps.
7. Pour the apricot filling into the sweet pastry base until approximately 5 mm from the top.
8. Using a piping bag and medium star piping tube, pipe the melting moment mixture (see recipe on next page) over the apricot filling in a trellis pattern.
9. Place directly into a preheated oven set at 180°C and bake for 30–40 minutes or until golden brown. Ensure that the sweet pastry base is completely baked.
10. Cool and carefully remove from the flan tin.
11. Once completely cool, dust or sprinkle the trellis top with icing sugar.

Melting Moment Topping

1. Place the icing sugar, butter and vanilla essence into a mixing bowl fitted with a beater, and beat until the mixture is very soft and fluffy, ensuring that you scrape the sides of the mixing bowl down during this stage. It is important that the butter and sugar mixture is well creamed and soft otherwise it will be difficult to pipe.
2. Sieve the flour and cornflour together and add to the creamed butter and sugar.
3. Beat until the dry ingredients are mixed in, but do not overmix.
4. Place into a piping bag and pipe immediately.

HELEN RICHARDS
MUFFIN TIME

*H*elen Richards came from a business background to start her muffin bakery in Dunedin. In 1990 she set up the retail outlet for her tasty muffins, which quickly won the approval of customers throughout the city and the South Island. In order to expand her business Helen worked extensively with the Otago University Food Science Department to develop a frozen muffin batter, which is marketed nationwide. The business has grown, producing an extremely high quality product, which has won two Carter Holt Harvey Food Awards.

Muffin Time's muffins are made with the best available ingredients, and a large selection of freshly baked muffins are enjoyed every day by customers.

Chocolate Ecstasy Muffins

Chocolate lovers will revel in these rich chocolate muffins that are layered with chocolate chips and chocolate buttons.

1. Place the butter in a large bowl, and microwave to melt.
2. Add eggs and milk, and mix well together.
3. Sieve the flour, baking powder, sugar and cocoa. Add the chocolate chips. Add to the liquid mixture.
4. Using a wooden spoon stir until all ingredients are just combined. Don't overmix.
5. Pour one third of the batter into greased muffin pans or 12 muffin paper cases.
6. Place a white chocolate button in each muffin mould.
7. Pour more batter on top of the chocolate button. Total batter weight in each mould is approximately 120 g.
8. Sprinkle with chocolate chips or place a milk chocolate button on top of each muffin.
9. Bake in a preheated oven set at 180°C for 20–25 minutes.
10. Remove from the tray while still warm.
11. Cool and dust with icing sugar.

115 g butter
75 g eggs (1^1/$_2$)
425 ml milk
450 g Champion or Elfin Standard Plain Flour
25 g baking powder
210 g granulated sugar
60 g cocoa
115 g chocolate chips

FILLING
white and milk chocolate buttons or chocolate chips
icing sugar to dust

Orange Cheesecake Muffins

Sweet and fruity, these orange flavoured muffins are quite refreshing. The cream cheese centre adds a smooth dimension to the crumbly texture.

1. Wash the oranges and remove half the zest. Quarter the oranges, removing any pips.
2. Place the orange quarters into a blender and blend for 15 seconds.
3. Add the chopped butter and blend for 30–60 seconds.
4. Add the egg and water, and blend for a further 2–3 minutes.
5. Pour the blended mixture into a large bowl.
6. Sieve the flour, sugar and baking powder, and add to the above.
7. Using a wooden spoon stir until all ingredients are just combined. Don't overmix.
8. Pour one third of the batter into greased muffin pans or 12 muffin paper cases.
9. Pipe or spoon approximately 15 g of softened cream cheese into each muffin mould.
10. Pour more batter on top of the cream cheese. Total batter weight in each mould is approximately 105 g.
11. Place a thinly sliced piece of orange on top of each muffin and sprinkle with a little granulated sugar.
12. Bake in a preheated oven set at 180°C for 20–25 minutes.
13. Remove from the tray while still warm.
14. Cool and brush with apricot glaze (see recipe for Mediterranean Orange Cake, page 119).

1^1/$_2$ medium fresh oranges
135 g softened butter
75 g eggs (1^1/$_2$)
240 g water
445 g Champion or Elfin Standard Plain Flour
215 g granulated sugar
20 g baking powder

FILLING
180 g cream cheese (approximately 15 g per muffin)

Spinach and Parmesan Muffins

A top seller at Muffin Time, this delicious savoury muffin is almost a meal. The cream cheese filling eliminates the need for butter, and provides a surprise in the centre.

240 ml milk

65 ml oil

95 g grated cheese

80 g parmesan cheese

135 g spinach (chopped well)

10 g chilli sauce

150 g eggs (3)

480 g Champion or Elfin Standard
  Plain Flour

20 g baking powder

pinch of salt

180 g cream cheese (approximately
  15 g per muffin)

sesame and pumpkin seeds

1. Place the milk, oil, grated and parmesan cheeses, spinach, chilli sauce and eggs into a large bowl and stir well.
2. Sieve the flour, baking powder and salt, and add to the above mixture.
3. Using a wooden spoon stir until all ingredients are just combined. Don't overmix.
4. Pour one third of the batter into greased muffin pans or 12 muffin paper cases.
5. Pipe or spoon approximately 15 g of softened cream cheese on top of each muffin.
6. Pour more batter on top of the cream cheese. Total batter weight in each mould is approximately 105 g.
7. Sprinkle the muffin batter with sesame and pumpkin seeds.
8. Bake in a preheated oven set at 180°C for 20–25 minutes.
9. Remove from the tray while still warm.

Maple Muffins (without egg)

The distinctive flavour of maple syrup shines through in these unusual muffins. Look for authentic maple syrup as there are some cheaper imitation maple syrups around that are more sugary and less nutty.

130 g softened butter

200 g granulated sugar

360 g Champion or Elfin Standard
  Plain Flour

20 g baking powder

pinch of salt

140 g rolled oats

240 g maple syrup

210 ml water

chopped walnuts (optional)

ICING

25 g softened butter

70 g maple syrup

150 g icing sugar

walnuts to garnish

1. Soften the butter in a microwave on low. Do not melt.
2. Add the sugar and beat until lightly creamed.
3. Sieve the flour, baking powder and salt, and add the rolled oats. Then add this to the creamed butter mixture.
4. Mix until the mixture resembles the consistency of coarse breadcrumbs.
5. Combine the maple syrup and water.
6. Add to the dry ingredients and mix until just combined. Don't overmix.
7. Pour batter into greased muffin pans or 12 muffin paper cases. Batter weight for each muffin should be approximately 105 g. Sprinkle chopped walnuts onto the batter if desired.
8. Bake in a preheated oven set at 180°C for 20–25 minutes.
9. Remove from the tray while still warm.
10. Cool before icing.

Maple Icing
1. Mix all ingredients well in a bowl.
2. Add a little milk if the icing is too firm.
3. Spread or pipe icing onto the cooled muffins.
4. Place half a walnut in the middle of the icing before it sets.

NADA BAKERY

Peter Gray (below) exemplifies the traditional, hard-working New Zealand baker. Following a humble Johnsonville childhood, he worked long hours to build his very successful bakery, Nada Cakes, and has worked equally hard for the New Zealand Baking Society. Currently president of the society, Peter has taken special interest in all aspects of the industry. He has overseen the formation of a buying group, which has led to wider training opportunities for apprentices, and the ongoing education and development of existing bakers.

He passionately believes that the status of the baker should be raised, and that the industry be proactive in education and research. He leads tours to the large baking shows of Europe and has been extremely innovative in organising training videos and fostering business plans for bakers.

His own bakery in his hometown of Johnsonville has a neverending stream of customers through the door, seeking special breads, pies and the mainstay of his business, specialty cakes. Peter has observed changes in Kiwi tastes in the past 20 years, and continues to develop baked products with less sugar, lower salt and gluten-free content.

Boiled Festive Fruit Cake

Easy to make, this sultana cake is a classic recipe from Nada. The boiling of the fruit ensures that the cake is moist and spicy. The recipe includes decoration of the top for festive occasions, especially Christmas.

1. Place the sultanas and ground ginger in a saucepan and just cover with water. Bring to the boil and simmer on a medium heat for 5 minutes. Drain in a large sieve and leave to cool. Reserve the juices.
2. Place the eggs, sugar, brandy, essence and reserved juice in a mixing bowl fitted with a beater. Beat together for 2 minutes on medium speed.
3. Sieve the flour and baking powder into a bowl. Place the butter in a bowl and melt in the microwave.
4. Add the cooled sultanas, melted butter and dry ingredients to the egg/sugar mixture.
5. Mix on medium speed for 1 minute until a smooth batter is formed, scrape down the sides of the bowl and mix for 20 seconds. Do not overmix.
6. Prepare a 20 cm round cake tin by lining the edges and bottom with greaseproof paper, two-ply thick.
7. Pour the batter into the tin and pat the mixture flat leaving a dip in the middle.
8. Place into a preheated oven (with a pan of water in it) at 140°C, and bake for $1\frac{3}{4}$ hours or until baked. Place a piece of greaseproof paper over the cake halfway through baking.
9. Leave in the tin to cool.
10. Remove from the tin and remove the greaseproof paper.
11. Brush the top surface of the cake with an apricot glaze (see Mediterranean Orange Cake, page 119). Decorate in a pattern with a variety of nuts, glacé cherries, crystallised fruit, etc.
12. Brush the nuts and glacé fruits with the apricot glaze. This seals the festive topping and gives a nice sheen.

CAKE

315 g sultanas
5 g ground ginger
water to just cover sultanas and ginger
125 g eggs ($2\frac{1}{2}$)
175 g soft brown sugar
5 ml brandy
280 g Champion or Elfin High Grade Flour
5 g baking powder
175 g melted butter (still warm)
2 drops almond essence

DECORATION

apricot glaze (see Mediterranean Orange Cake, page 119)
assorted nuts, e.g., pecans, brazil, blanched whole almonds, walnuts, etc.
red and green glacé cherries
crystallised fruits, e.g., pineapple, ginger, etc.

German Baked Cheesecake

Sitting on a sweet pastry base, this light baked cheesecake has a delicious lemony tang. It is a classic bakery item.

PASTRY

170 g salted butter

85 g sugar

50 g egg (1)

260 g Champion or Elfin Standard
  Plain Flour

FILLING

150 g cream cheese

150 g sour cream

pinch of salt

50 g Champion or Elfin High
  Grade Flour

45 g milk powder

100 g caster sugar

75 g (1$\frac{1}{2}$) warmed eggs

75 g melted butter

zest and juice of $\frac{1}{2}$ lemon

Sweet Pastry Base

1. Lightly cream the butter and sugar in a mixing bowl fitted with a beater or beat in a bowl with a wooden spoon.
2. Add the egg and mix until combined.
3. Lastly add the flour and mix to a paste. Only mix until the paste comes clean off the bowl. Be careful not to overmix or the pastry will become too elastic.
4. Transfer to a bowl, cover and refrigerate for 30 minutes or overnight.
5. On a lightly floured workbench roll the pastry out into a sheet about 4–5 mm thick, and big enough to cover a 25 cm greased fluted loose bottomed flan tin.
6. Use the rolling pin to pick the pastry up and lay it over the tin. Gently press the pastry into the tin so that it fills all the contours. Be careful not to stretch the pastry or it will tear, or shrink back in the oven. Return it to the fridge for another 30 minutes, or more if the pastry still feels soft. Reserve the scraps.

Filling

1. Place the cream cheese in a mixing bowl and microwave on low heat for 1 minute. Add the sour cream. Beat with a beater until well combined and smooth.
2. Sieve the salt, flour, milk powder and caster sugar together and add to the cheese mixture. Beat on medium speed for 5 minutes.
3. Continue beating and slowly add the warmed eggs and melted butter. Lastly add the lemon zest and juice. Mix until smooth, approximately 1 minute.
4. Pour the mixture into the prepared lined flan tin and level the mixture.
5. Place into a preheated oven set at 160°C and bake for 45 minutes or until just set.
6. Allow the cheesecake to cool slightly before removing from the tin. When removing the cheesecake from the tin, place the tin on a small drinking glass or cup and allow the rim to fall away.

KAYE AND RICHARD TOLLENAAR

PANDORO BAKERY

Authentic Italian artisan breads and cakes are the passion of this talented couple who operate a busy Parnell store and two large wholesale bakeries in Auckland and Wellington. Kaye was inspired to bake handcrafted breads while cooking alongside visiting chef Tony Papas at a Parnell restaurant in the early 90s. As newlyweds, Kaye and Richard Tollenaar opened Pandoro Panetteria and within six weeks the bakery was at maximum capacity, forcing them to open a wholesale plant to cater for the unprecedented demand.

They travel the world in search of new breads, ideas and techniques and have almost traded places in the management of the company. While it is Kaye's expertise that got them up and running, Richard has developed a passion for baking that now sees him at the helm of the production, while Kaye manages the business details. Richard travelled to the Culinary Institute of America to spend a week with some of the USA's top artisan bakers and has a newfound fascination with tasty sourdoughs and artisan-style organic loaves that are popular lines with their customers.

Pandoro breads are sought by foodlovers, top restaurants and even airlines because the best possible ingredients are used, and there is no compromise in production. The shelves are crammed with a large variety of rustic-looking breads and rolls, toothsome European cakes and biscotti which are baked each day. No artificial flavourings, extenders or preservatives are used, which means that their bread is best eaten the day it is bought.

Kaye and Richard are as passionate about their craft as it is possible to be. They manage to juggle their businesses with their family of two young daughters, while continually seeking out potential new products and developing an even greater range of delicious breads and cakes.

Mediterranean Orange Cake

A moist cake that is perfect as a light dessert or with coffee. The orange slush should be made ahead, preferably a day before, and refrigerated.

Orange Slush

1. Wash the oranges, then cut off the tops and bottoms and place in a large pot.
2. Fill with enough water to cover half the oranges, and simmer uncovered for 2 hours.
3. Drain off the excess water, place the oranges in a food processor and purée.
4. Place in a bowl and cover; refrigerate overnight.

Cake

1. Prepare a 23 cm tin by greasing and lining the bottom and sides with baking paper. Preheat the oven to 170°C.
2. Mix the baking powder and ground almonds together to ensure even dispersal of the baking powder within the cake.
3. Mix the eggs and sugar together until just combined. Be careful not beat the eggs as this will aerate the mixture.
4. Add the orange slush and baking powder mixture, then mix gently until well combined.
5. Pour the mixture into the tin and bake for approximately 80 minutes.
6. Cool overnight in the tin, covered loosely with plastic wrap.
7. The next day remove the baking paper and place on a wire cooling rack.
8. Using a pastry brush, brush the entire cake (excluding the bottom) with apricot glaze (see recipe below), ensuring an even, glossy finish.
9. Toast natural flaked almonds on a baking tray, in a oven set at 200°C, until light amber. Keep a close eye on the almonds as they colour quickly. Cool before use.
10. Gently sprinkle the toasted almonds around the top edge of the cake, creating a ring of toasted almonds approximately 2.5 cm wide.

Apricot Glaze

1. Mix apricot jam and water together in a saucepan.
2. Bring to the boil, but do not boil too long as this will evaporate the water.
3. Once boiled, pass through a sieve to remove any lumps or coarse apricot pulp.
4. Use hot, reheating if necessary in the microwave.

Note: the consistency can be adjusted with water.

SLUSH
4 oranges
water

CAKE
15 g baking powder
310 g ground blanched almonds
400 g eggs (8)
310 g caster sugar
375 g orange slush (see above)
natural flaked almonds for decoration

GLAZE
300 g apricot jam
150 g water

Citron Tart

A real favourite at Pandoro, this tart is filled with melt-in-the-mouth tangy lemon cream that will appeal to everyone.

PASTRY

170 g salted butter

85 g sugar

50 g egg (1)

260 g Champion or Elfin Standard Plain Flour

FILLING

3 fresh lemons

350 g eggs (7)

300 g caster sugar

240 ml fresh cream

Sweet Pastry

1. Lightly cream the butter and sugar in a mixing bowl fitted with a beater or beat in a bowl with a wooden spoon.
2. Add the egg and mix until combined.
3. Lastly add the flour and mix to a paste. Only mix until the paste comes clean off the bowl. Be careful not to overmix or the pastry will become too elastic.
4. Transfer to a bowl, cover and refrigerate for 30 minutes or overnight.
5. On a lightly floured workbench roll the pastry out into a sheet about 5 mm thick, and big enough to cover a 28 cm greased flan or tart tin.
6. Use the rolling pin to pick the pastry up and lay it over the tin. Gently press the pastry into the tin so that it fills all the contours. Be careful not to stretch the pastry or it will tear, or shrink back in the oven, causing the filling to leak or spill. Return it to the fridge for another 30 minutes, or more if the pastry still feels soft. Reserve the scraps for later.
7. Preheat the oven to 150°C. Line the pastry with tinfoil and fill with dried beans, raw rice or pastry weights.
8. Bake the pastry for 30 minutes. It should be baked but not coloured.
9. Allow the pastry to cool before checking for any cracks or holes. Also make sure the pastry has not shrunk on the sides. Patch any low points, holes or cracks with your leftover pastry.

The Citron Mix

This can be prepared while you wait for the pastry to rest or bake, but you will get better results if the mix is made a day in advance and refrigerated overnight.

1. Wash the lemons in warm water. Zest and squeeze out their juice.
2. Combine the eggs and sugar and mix gently until the sugar is dissolved.
3. Lightly beat the cream with a whisk, then add the egg mixture and stir to combine.
4. Add the juice and zest. Stir only until slightly thickened (1–2 minutes).
5. Transfer the citron mix to a container and rest in the fridge, preferably overnight.
6. Preheat the oven to 170°C. Pour the citron mix into the patched pastry case.
7. Bake for 40–50 minutes until a nice golden brown and set. Cool before removing from the tin.

Pane Acido (Organic Sourdough Starter)

Pane acido is the Italian sourdough starter (the French refer to this as a leaven), however, they both serve the same purpose and are largely used in the production of sourdough-based breads. The difference between a biga and pane acido is the biga contains a percentage of commercial baker's yeast, whereas the pane acido relies on capturing the wild yeasts in the air.

Sourdough is both the oldest and newest way of making bread. Thousands of years ago people noticed that their porridge-like mixtures of flour and water started to bubble when left for a few days. Over time they learnt how to control this activity and use it to make bread – a universal staple. Until commercial yeast was discovered in the late 18th century, sourdough was the only way of baking. In the last 20 to 30 years these old methods have been revived and refined, resulting in more consistent products produced on a commercial scale – albeit only by dedicated bakers!

Capturing the Wild Yeast

DAY ONE
Equipment:
1 large bowl
1 piece of muslin cloth

400 g stoneground organic flour
500 ml filtered water (about 25°C)

Mix the flour and water together to a smooth batter in the bowl. The temperature of the water is important. If it is too cold, the yeasts will lie dormant. If it is too hot, they will die. Cover the bowl with the muslin and place somewhere outside where it will get plenty of fresh air, but no direct sunlight.

DAY TWO
Twenty-four hours later, some bubbles may appear on the surface. This is a good sign. Use a wooden spoon to beat air into the mixture, cover with the muslin and leave for another 24 hours.

Breeding the Yeasts

DAYS THREE AND FOUR
If there are no bubbles by day three you should start again. Assuming there is some activity, it's now time to bring the culture inside and increase the concentration of yeasts. To do this, feed the culture with:

200 ml **filtered water (about 25°C)**
200 g **stoneground organic flour**

Pour the water in first and break up the culture in the water. This helps disperse the yeast spores throughout the liquid. Then add the flour and mix well. Don't worry about it being a bit lumpy as that will all go as the yeasts ferment. Cover the bowl with the muslin again and let it stand in a warm place. (In summertime almost anywhere is fine. In winter try on top of the fridge, or somewhere else that gets to about 23–25°C.) Leave the starter about 24 hours before feeding it again with the same quantities of flour and water.

There is a risk from this point on that mould may appear. All this means is that the balance of yeasts and lacto-bacteria needs to be corrected. Scrape off any hairy bits from the starter, transfer to a clean bowl, and give it another feed. This will encourage more yeasts to multiply.

DAYS FIVE AND SIX

As the yeast spores multiply they start getting through their food a bit quicker, so you need to feed them more regularly. About 12 hours after the last feeding on day four, you should pour off half the culture, and feed the remainder with the same quantities of flour and water as above. Twelve hours later feed the culture again. The next day, pour off half the culture and feed twice, as you did on day five.

Feeding the Yeasts

Having captured the yeasts, you now need to keep them alive. This is where having a sourdough starter becomes a bit like owning a pet. Yeast needs to eat three times a day if it is to perform well.

DAY SEVEN ONWARD

Equipment:

starter container with lid (with a small air-hole in the lid)

rubber spatula (or a keen pair of hands)

FIRST FEED

100 g starter (discard the rest)

50 g stoneground organic flour

50 ml water (25°C)

Allow to ferment for about eight hours.

SECOND FEED

200 g starter

100 g stoneground organic flour

100 ml water (25°C)

Allow to ferment for about eight hours.

THIRD FEED

400 g starter

200 g stoneground organic flour

200 ml water (25°C)

Allow the starter to ferment for eight hours before starting again with the first feed. After a couple of weeks, if all has gone well, you should have a happy and healthy sourdough starter. From about day 10 it will be strong enough to make bread, and this strength will increase as your starter matures. As your starter ages it will develop consistency, balance and, to a certain extent, immunity from foreign invaders.

The difference between sourdough and regular bread is basically in the yeast. Commercial, or baker's yeast, is a particular strain that is hybridised to ferment quickly and consistently. Sourdoughs utilise wild yeast spores present in grain flours, fruits, vegetables, or in the air. Before making bread the yeasts need to be captured, bred and fed in order to get as many of them as you can into enough of a feeding frenzy to leaven the bread. These yeasts work a lot slower than their high-speed commercial cousins, but the resulting bread has a much better flavour, texture, aroma and keeping qualities. Many books recommend that only advanced or experienced bakers attempt to make sourdough. All you really need, though, is enthusiasm and dedication. Remember, our ancestors used this method in their homes centuries ago, and thought nothing of it.

The Feeding Schedule

The timing of your feeding schedule can be organised to suit your day, and your baking plans. I prefer to make my dough first thing in the morning, so my feeding schedule looks something like this:

8 am	*first feed*	*}*
4 pm	*second feed*	*} the days before baking*
10 pm	*third feed*	*}*
6 am	*make dough*	

However, if you wanted to bake your bread late at night, you might try something like this:

2 pm	*first feed*	*}*
10 pm	*second feed*	*} the days before baking*
7 am	*third feed*	*}*
3 pm	*make dough*	

If you are just maintaining your starter, but not planning to make bread, throwing out nearly a kilogram of starter every day may seem quite wasteful. And it is. Once your starter is bubbling along in a healthy way (at least two weeks after day one), you can store it in the fridge while you are not using it. This should be done just after the first feed, so the yeast has some food for its hibernation. In the fridge most of the yeasts will go dormant, just snoozing until you wake them up. As time goes on, though, these dormant spores will start to die off. So while the starter is in cold storage it will still need the occasional feed. This can be done once a week, with the same amounts as for normal feeding (discarding the excess as required), but with slightly warmer water (about 35°C). This will allow the yeasts to feed for a while before going dormant in the cold again.

A word of warning, though: you will need to get the starter back on three feeds a day at room temperature at least two days before you bake with it again. If you try to make bread with starter straight from the fridge you will fail.

Organic Sourdough Bread

Although a lot of effort, this bread is a very rewarding experience. The loaf is full of flavour, with a great chewy crust. Take time to read the notes on the organic sourdough starter (pane acido).

1. Sieve the flour onto your work surface. Make a well and add the pane acido and water, mixing well as you would for the feeding of the pane acido.
2. Mix or knead the dough by hand using the technique shown in the All About Breads section. Continue kneading until the ingredients are well combined (the dough is not fully developed at this stage).
3. Put the dough into a bowl, and cover with plastic. Leave for 20 minutes to rest. (This rest is called autolysis and it is an extremely useful baking trick. Allowing the dough to rest without salt is achieving a number of desirable ends. First, the flour, without salt, absorbs water faster, resulting in a moister, springier loaf. Second, as the dough rests the fermentation begins. A side-effect of fermentation is gluten development, which is what we are trying to achieve by mixing the dough in the first place. The good thing about the autolysis is that the gluten is developed very gently. Finally, as the dough ferments it relaxes and softens, making it easier to knead.)
4. Add the sea salt.
5. Continue to knead the dough by hand. Every couple of minutes stop and check the gluten development and temperature of the dough. This final kneading should take about 10–15 minutes (check if you have fully developed the dough by using the stretch test).
6. Lightly oil a bowl large enough to allow the dough to double in bulk. Put the dough in the bowl and cover with plastic. Leave in a warmish place (23–25°C) for 3 hours. By this time the dough should be nearly double in size.
7. Gently knock back the dough in the bowl. This will deflate it slightly. Cover again and leave for another 60 minutes, by which time it should have well and truly doubled. After baking a few times you will know the feel of a dough that has fermented fully.
8. Tip the dough out onto a lightly floured bench and using a dough scraper cut the dough in half. Be gentle with the dough; do not aggressively punch it down, or squeeze all the gas from within. Pick each piece up and gently tuck the edges underneath, pulling the surface tight around the mass. Lay the pieces back on the floured bench and cover with a proofing cloth (or tea towel). Give an intermediate proof of 20 minutes. While you wait, lightly dust two round proofing baskets with rye flour.
9. Uncover the dough and shape each piece into a ball by cupping your hands around and moving in a circular motion, pulling the skin tight over the dough. Don't overdo it though, or the skin will rip and this will spoil the appearance of the finished product. The final shape will look like a smooth ball, but with a rough, scrunched-up bottom. This is called the seam. When the shaping is complete, place the breads in the proofing baskets, seam up. Cover the baskets with plastic or a proofing cloth, and leave in a warm, draught-free place, to rise.

1 kg organic white flour
300 g organic sourdough starter (see pane acido)
600 ml filtered water
20 g sea salt

Finished dough temperature: 24°C

10. Final proof for approximately $2^1/_2$–3 hours. Cover with plastic to prevent skinning and chilling of the dough. Use the indentation test to tell when the dough is three-quarters proofed.

11. The oven should be preheated to 240°C, with a baking stone in place. Gently tip one loaf out onto a peel lightly dusted with semolina. The seam that was on the top is now on the bottom.

12. Using a razor blade or sharp knife, score the top of the loaf.

13. Just before you load the bread into the oven, spray water into the oven cavity. Close the door quickly so you don't lose any of the steam.

14. With the peel and loaf in one hand, open the oven with the other, and gently 'flick' the loaf off the peel and onto the baking stone. Close the oven door immediately.

15. Repeat this for the second loaf, but be careful not to spray water directly onto the first loaf. Close the door again and wait 2 minutes before opening the door slightly and spraying more water into the oven. Two minutes later, 'steam' the oven again. Resist opening the door for another 20 minutes.

16. Turn the heat down to 220°C, and check the loaves for even baking. If necessary, turn them around. For the remaining baking time leave the door of the oven slightly ajar to thicken and dry the crust (remember to tap the bottom of the loaf; if it sounds hollow it is baked).

17. After 30–35 minutes the loaves will be ready. Cool on a wire rack.

Note: the organic flour can be replaced with Champion or Elfin High Grade Flour. However, the final proof will be up to 1 hour longer and the water level should be reduced to 560 ml.

Pane Italiano

A crusty white loaf that is made by the biga or sponge method. Not to be confused with sourdough, pane Italiano is made with commercial yeast, but unlike most commercial yeasted breads, this method results in a very flavourful bread with great texture that keeps quite well.

DAY ONE (AT ABOUT 9 PM)

The Biga

1. In a large bowl dissolve the dried yeast and honey in the warm water, then add the flour and knead roughly together by hand (do not over knead at this stage).
2. Cover with plastic and leave to ferment overnight.

DAY TWO (AT ABOUT 9 AM)

The Dough

1. Sieve the flour and semolina onto your work surface. Make a well and add the biga or sponge.
2. In a bowl, dissolve the yeast in the water. Add the water and yeast to the well.
3. Mix or knead the dough by hand using the technique shown in the All About Bread section. Continue kneading until the ingredients are well combined (the dough is not fully developed at this stage).
4. Put the dough into a bowl, and cover with plastic. Leave the dough for 20 minutes to rest.
5. Add the sea salt.
6. Continue to knead the dough by hand. Every couple of minutes stop and check the gluten development and temperature of the dough. This final kneading should take about 10–15 minutes (check if you have fully developed the dough by using the stretch test).
7. Lightly oil a bowl large enough to allow the dough to double in bulk. Put the dough in the bowl and cover with plastic. Leave in a warmish place (23–25°C) for 30 minutes. By this time the dough should be nearly double in size.
8. Gently knock back the dough in the bowl. This will deflate it slightly. Cover again and leave for another 30 minutes, then knock it back again. After resting in the bowl for another 30–40 minutes the dough should be fully fermented.
9. Tip the dough out onto a lightly floured bench and using a dough scraper cut the dough in half. Be gentle with the dough; do not aggressively punch it down, or squeeze all the gas from within. Pick each piece up and gently tuck the edges underneath, pulling the surface tight around the mass. Lay the pieces back on the floured bench and cover with a proofing cloth (or tea towel). Give an intermediate proof of 10 minutes. While you wait, lightly dust a proofing cloth or tea towel with rye flour.
10. Uncover the dough and mould each piece into a vienna or baton shape. The surface of the dough should be stretched tightly over the mass, and there should be a neat seam along one side. Lay the first loaf on the proofing cloth, seam up, and then shape the second loaf in the same way. Before laying the second loaf down pleat the cloth so that the loaves cannot touch as they rise.

BIGA
1 g Elfin Dried Yeast (¹/₄ tsp from sachet, keep unopened sachet in the refrigerator)
10 g honey
250 ml water
250 g Champion or Elfin High Grade Flour

DOUGH
500 g Champion or Elfin High Grade Flour
50 g semolina
biga or sponge from day before
7 g Elfin Dried Yeast (balance of the sachet)
250 ml water
10 g sea salt

Finished dough temperature: 27°C

11. Final proof for approximately 45–60 minutes in a warm, draught-free place. Cover with plastic to prevent skinning and chilling of the dough. Use the indentation test to tell when the dough is three-quarters proofed.

12. The oven should be preheated to 220°C, with a baking stone in place. Gently tip one loaf out onto a peel lightly dusted with semolina. The seam that was on the top is now on the bottom.

13. Using a razor blade or sharp knife, slash a single, long, deep 45° cut in the top of the loaf (see diagram).

14. Just before you load the bread into the oven, spray water into the oven cavity. Close the door quickly so you don't lose any of the steam.

15. With the peel and loaf in one hand, open the oven with the other, and gently 'flick' the loaf off the peel and onto the baking stone. Close the oven door immediately.

16. Repeat this for the second loaf, but be careful not to spray water directly onto the first loaf. Close the door again and wait 2 minutes before opening the door slightly and spraying more water into the oven. Two minutes later, 'steam' the oven again. Resist opening the door for another 20 minutes.

17. Turn the heat down to 200°C, and check the loaves for even baking. If necessary, turn them around. For the remaining time leave the door of the oven slightly ajar to thicken and dry the crust.

18. After 30–35 minutes the loaves will be ready. Cool on a wire rack.

Olive Bread

Almost a meal by itself, this decorative bread has a fragrant, sweet onion jam filling. Choose full-flavoured olives for the best taste, and serve this bread warm.

16 g Elfin Dried Yeast (2 sachets)

275 g water

500 g Champion or Elfin High
 Grade Flour

10 g salt

10 g olive oil

70 g pitted sliced olives

150 g onion jam (see recipe opposite)

1 sprig fresh rosemary

rock salt

olive oil

Finished dough temperature: 28°C

1. In a small bowl dissolve the yeast in the warm water. Let stand for 10 minutes.
2. Sieve the flour onto your work surface and make a well. Add the salt and olive oil.
3. Mix or knead the dough by hand using the technique shown in the All About Bread section. Continue to knead the dough by hand. Every couple of minutes stop and check the gluten development and temperature of the dough. This final kneading should take about 10–15 minutes (check if you have fully developed the dough by using the stretch test).
4. Add the well-drained olives and continue mixing until the olives are evenly distributed.
5. Lightly oil a bowl large enough to allow the dough to double in bulk. Put the dough in the bowl and cover with plastic. Leave in a warmish place (23–25°C) to ferment for 30–40 minutes.
6. Gently knock back the dough after 25 minutes, cover with plastic again. By this time the dough should be nearly double in size.
7. Tip the dough out onto the bench, which has been lightly dusted with flour.
8. Using a dough scraper, divide the dough in half (400 g each piece).
9. Shape each piece into a ball or cob shape.
10. Place on a lightly floured bench and give an intermediate proof of 10 minutes, covered with plastic.
11. Using a rolling pin, roll each ball out into a long, flat, oval shape.
12. Place 75 g of onion jam and a few rosemary leaves slightly off centre on the dough (see diagram).
13. Fold the dough over and pinch the edges together.
14. Lightly brush the top with olive oil and smear 35 g of onion jam all over the top surface. Sprinkle with a few more rosemary leaves and some rock salt to finish.
15. Bend slightly to form a crescent shape and pinch along the edge to scallop shape the bread.
16. Place the two dough pieces on a lightly greased baking tray, allowing enough room for the dough to almost double in size.
17. Final proof for 30–40 minutes in a warm, draught-free place. Do not overproof.
18. The oven should be preheated to 220°C. Place the baking tray into the oven and steam the oven.
19. Bake for 20–25 minutes until golden brown. Avoid excessive oven heat and baking time as this will burn the onion jam.
20. Remove from the oven and brush immediately with olive oil.
21. Cool on a wire rack.

Onion Jam (filling for the olive bread)

Onion jam is great on an antipasto platter or served with a steak. Otherwise it can be used as a filling in olive bread, making this loaf virtually a meal in itself.

1. Heat the oil and add the onion, bayleaves and rosemary.
2. Brown well over a low-medium heat, stirring regularly to prevent sticking.
3. Add the vinegar and stir well to deglaze the pan.
4. Finally, add the sugar and mustard seeds and cook over a low heat, covered, for about 30 minutes.
5. The finished product should be quite thick and a shiny, rich brown. Cool completely before using to fill the olive bread.

Note: the onion jam can be made in advance and kept in an airtight container for 2–3 days in the refrigerator.

2 tablespoons olive oil

3 medium onions, chopped

2 bayleaves

1 sprig fresh rosemary

2 tablespoons red wine vinegar (balsamic is even better)

50 g brown sugar

1 tablespoon yellow mustard seeds

1 tablespoon black mustard seeds

Panettone

Soft, sweet and yeasty, this light Italian bread is traditionally served at Christmas time. It originated in the 15th century and has become a sought after gift in the festive season. It is delicious grilled or lightly toasted and spread with butter.

SPONGE

11 g Elfin Dried Yeast (part of 2 sachets)

115 ml water (25°C)

100 g Champion or Elfin High Grade Flour

25 g caster sugar

50 g eggs (1)

FIRST DOUGH

5 g Elfin Dried Yeast (balance of the 2 sachets)

15 ml water (25°C)

500 g Champion or Elfin High Grade Flour

50 g caster sugar

100 g eggs (2)

55 g softened butter

SECOND DOUGH

200 g eggs (4)

2 egg yolks

185 g granulated sugar

15 g liquid honey

5 ml vanilla essence

zest of one lemon

285 g softened butter

350 g Champion or Elfin High Grade Flour

5 g salt

75 g candied citron or mixed peel

170 g raisins (washed and well-drained)

whole blanched almonds to garnish

PASTE

2 egg whites

15 g caster sugar

115 g icing sugar (sieved)

65 g ground almonds

The Sponge

1. In a large bowl dissolve the yeast in the water. Let stand for 10 minutes.
2. Mix in the flour, caster sugar and egg. Knead to form a smooth dough (this will not take long).
3. Cover with plastic and leave to ferment for 30 minutes.

First Dough

1. In a small bowl dissolve the yeast in the water. Let stand for 10 minutes.
2. Sieve the flour onto your work surface. Make a well. Add the sugar, eggs, sponge and yeast mixture.
3. Mix or knead the dough by hand using the technique shown in the All About Bread section. Continue to knead the dough by hand until three-quarters of the dough development has been achieved.
4. Add the softened butter in small additions, kneading well between each. Once the butter has been kneaded in, you should have a smooth, silky, well-developed dough.
5. Lightly oil a bowl large enough to allow the dough to double in bulk. Put the dough in the bowl and cover with plastic. Leave in a warmish place (23–25°C) to ferment for 30–40 minutes.

Second Dough

1. Add the eggs, egg yolks, sugar, honey, vanilla essence and lemon zest to the first dough and beat in using a wooden spoon.
2. Gradually mix in the softened butter, then add the flour and salt.
3. Knead the dough until you have achieved a smooth, silky, well-developed dough (6–8 minutes).
4. Mix the candied citron and raisins with a small dusting of flour to help separate them and absorb a little of the moisture and mix in to the dough. Avoid excessive kneading as this will cause the raisins to break up and discolour the dough. **Note:** this dough will be soft and sticky.
5. Lightly oil a bowl large enough to allow the dough to double in bulk. Put the dough in the bowl and cover with plastic. Leave in a warmish place (23–25°C) to ferment for $2\frac{1}{2}$–3 hours.
6. Tip the dough out onto a lightly floured bench and using a dough scraper cut the dough in half. Be gentle with the dough; do not aggressively punch it down, or squeeze all the gas from within. Pick each piece up and gently tuck the edges underneath, pulling the surface tight around the mass.
7. Mould into a tightly round ball.
8. Place directly into a well-greased large catering can (size A10) or specialised panettone baking cup (available from specialist kitchen shops, see Sources, page 162).

9. Cover and leave to proof or until the dough has doubled in size, approximately 2–3 hours, depending on the temperature of the room. Use the indentation test to tell when the dough is fully proofed. Do not overproof.
10. Make the macaroon paste while the dough is proving (see recipe below).
11. Gently spread the macaroon paste onto the fully proofed panettone and decorate with a few whole blanched almonds. It is important to do this just before baking.
12. Place the panettone into a preheated oven set at 180°C and bake for 30 minutes. Then reduce the heat to 150°C and bake for a further 20 minutes.
13. Leave the panettone in their tins until they have cooled completely, or, if using the special panettone baking cups leave them in their cups until serving.
14. Wrap in cellophane and tie a bow around the top.

Macaroon Paste

1. Ensure all equipment is free from any traces of grease when making this mixture.
2. Whisk the egg whites until half risen.
3. Add the sugar and whisk until 'stiff peaks' form.
4. Sieve the icing sugar and ground almonds together and gently fold into the meringue. Mix until smooth. Avoid excessive mixing.

REMBRANDTS

Rembrandts patisserie in the busy affluent suburb of Remuera in Auckland sparkles with glass cases and mirrors that show off Peter Rood's fine chocolate and patisserie work. Peter is one of a handful of chocolatiers in New Zealand who make handmade European-style chocolates using the finest imported chocolate. His dainty morsels sit beside fine patisserie work that has earned him several gold medals.

Like many bakers, Peter grew up to his trade, and is a fifth generation baker. In fact, there are presently 35 bakers in his family, who have fanned out across the world to ply their craft. Peter opened his patisserie in 1997 and designed the kitchen, with its specialist areas for baking and chocolate work, himself. He is on a planned growth curve with plenty of room for expansion, and is currently training an apprentice.

Easter and Christmas are the busiest times at Rembrandts for there is a real demand for his superb chocolate eggs, novelties and cakes. This is a true specialty bakery with rows of mouthwatering chocolates, neat patisserie and delectable cakes and gateaux.

Almond Round – Gevulde Koeken

Halfway between a cake and a biscuit, these little almond rounds are found all over Europe. The strong almond flavour makes them a delight to eat, and they will keep for a week or two if stored in an airtight tin.

Biscuit Dough

1. Lightly cream the butter and sugar in a mixing bowl fitted with a beater or beat in a bowl with a wooden spoon (do not over cream the butter and sugar).
2. Add the egg and lemon juice and mix until combined.
3. Lastly add the sieved flour, salt and baking soda, and mix until the paste comes clean off the bowl. Be careful not to overmix or the pastry will become too elastic and doughy.
4. Transfer to a bowl. Cover and refrigerate for 30 minutes or overnight.
5. On a lightly floured workbench roll the pastry out into a sheet about 3–4 mm thick. Using a 7 cm crinkled round pastry cutter, cut 12 round discs out and place on a lightly greased or baking paper lined baking tray, ensuring that there is enough space between each biscuit – approximately 2 cm.
6. Using the same biscuit dough at the same thickness, cut a further 12 round discs, this time using an 8 cm crinkled round pastry cutter. Set aside.
7. Place the almond filling (see recipe below) into a piping bag fitted with a plain piping tube. Pipe a thin layer of almond filling onto the 7 cm discs (approximately 25 g per biscuit).
8. Lay the 8 cm discs on top of the biscuit base and almond filling and gently press the edges down to seal. Using a fork dipped in flour can assist in sealing the edges down by gently applying pressure to the top biscuit dough.
9. Using a pastry brush lightly egg wash (using the two beaten egg yolks) the top of the biscuit dough.
10. Lightly press one whole blanched almond in the centre of each biscuit, and glaze again using the same egg wash.
11. Place directly into a preheated oven set at 205°C and bake for 12–14 minutes until golden brown.
12. Allow to cool slightly; remove using a palette knife and place on a wire cooling rack.

Almond Filling

1. Mix all ingredients together to form a spreadable filling. This almond filling should not be firm, because it is to be piped through a piping bag.

Note: this almond filling will keep in the refrigerator for 2 weeks if stored in an airtight container.

DOUGH
150 g butter
125 g caster sugar
25 g egg ($^1/_2$)
5 ml lemon juice
250 g Champion or Elfin Standard Plain Flour
good pinch of salt
good pinch of baking soda
2 egg yolks, beaten
12 whole blanched almonds

FILLING
130 g ground almonds
130 g granulated sugar
25 g egg ($^1/_2$) (variable)
1–2 drops almond essence (optional)

Almond Filling
Biscuit Dough

Stollen

Traditionally baked at Christmas, this fruity, spicy bread is somewhat reminiscent of a brioche dough. The interior reveals a rich almond paste and the stollen has a shelf life of up to two weeks. For a perfect Christmas gift, wrap in cellophane and tie with a Christmas bow and ribbon.

FRUIT PREPARATION

150 g sultanas

95 g currants

40 g mixed peel

40 g chopped red cherries

50 g split almonds

40 g chopped walnuts

40 ml rum

100 g Champion or Elfin High Grade
   Flour (for later use)

FERMENT

165 g Champion or Elfin High
   Grade Flour

10g Elfin Dried Yeast

135 ml water

Finished dough temperature: 29°C

DOUGH

200 g Champion or Elfin High Grade
   Flour

60 g granulated sugar

5 g salt

80 g softened butter

2–3 drops vanilla essence

2–3 drops lemon essence

5 g nutmeg

5 g mixed spice

50 g (1) egg

icing sugar for dusting

ALMOND PASTE

75 g ground almonds

75 g granulated sugar

15 g egg ($^1/_4$) (variable)

1–2 drops almond essence (optional)

Day one: the fruit preparation

1. Place the sultanas and currants in a mixing bowl. Cover with warm water and soak for 1 hour.
2. Drain well in a sieve.
3. Add the mixed peel, red cherries, split almonds, walnuts and rum and mix together.
4. Cover with plastic wrap and stand for 24 hours.

Day two: the ferment

1. Mix all the flour, yeast and water to form a well-developed dough. This should take 5–8 minutes kneading by hand.
2. Lightly oil a bowl and place the developed dough into it. Cover with plastic wrap.
3. Leave in warm place to ferment for 25 minutes or until double in size.

Day two: the dough

1. Place all the ingredients in a mixing bowl fitted with a beater.
2. Cream together for 5–10 minutes on medium speed. Scrape the sides of the bowl down.
3. Add the ferment and mix in until clear and well combined. Scrape down the sides of the bowl.
4. Place the 100 g of flour into the soaked fruit and evenly toss the fruit until it is well coated.
5. Add the fruit to the ferment/batter mixture and mix the dough until clear and well combined. **Note:** the dough will be very tacky and soft, so use plenty of dusting flour to stop the dough from sticking to everything.
6. Divide the dough in half (575 g) and gently mould into an oblong shape, 18 cm in length.
7. Give an intermediate proof of 5–10 minutes with the seam facing upwards. Cover with plastic or a clean tea towel.
8. Flatten slightly and make an impression with a rolling pin slightly off centre.
9. Place a rope of almond paste (see recipe opposite) into the impression. Fold the short side over the almond rope and seal the two edges firmly.
10. Place onto a lightly greased or baking paper lined baking tray.
11. Proof in a warm place for 20–30 minutes. Do not give excessive proof time as the dough may collapse during the baking cycle.
12. Place directly into a preheated oven set at 200°C for 20–30 minutes.
13. When baked remove from the oven and place onto a wire rack. Using a pastry brush, brush liberally with melted butter while still hot.

14. Allow to cool slightly and then place in the refrigerator to set the butter. Remove after 30 minutes.
15. Just before serving dust heavily with icing sugar.

Almond paste
1. Mix all the ingredients together to form a firm paste.
2. Divide the mix in half and roll into a sausage shape.
3. Wrap in plastic wrap until required.

Note: this almond paste will keep in the refrigerator for two weeks if stored in an airtight container.

Oma's Dutch Apple Tart

This is a traditional Dutch recipe for a delicious apple tart. 'Oma' is the Dutch word for grandmother and this tart reflects the love of baking and passion that the Dutch have for family occasions. Serve with whipped cream for a real dessert treat.

PASTRY

300 g butter

150 g caster sugar

25 g egg ($^1/_2$)

5 ml lemon juice

*450 g Champion or Elfin Standard
    Plain Flour*

5 g salt

FILLING

*5 Granny Smith apples, peeled, cored
    and sliced*

100 g sultanas

50 g apricot jam

100 g white sponge or cake crumbs

100 g cold custard (see recipe below)

$^1/_2$ tablespoon lemon juice

5 g cinnamon

CUSTARD

75 ml milk

10 g sugar

25 ml milk

10 g Edmonds Custard Powder

GLAZE

300 g apricot jam

150 g water

Tart Dough

1. Lightly cream the butter and sugar in a mixing bowl fitted with a beater or beat in a bowl with a wooden spoon (do not over cream the butter and sugar).
2. Add the egg and lemon juice and mix until combined.
3. Lastly add the flour and salt, and mix until the paste comes clean off the bowl. Be careful not to overmix or the pastry will become too elastic and doughy.
4. Transfer to a bowl. Cover and refrigerate for 30 minutes or overnight.
5. On a lightly floured workbench roll the pastry out into a sheet about 4 mm thick, and big enough to cover a 23 cm greased, deep, loose bottomed tart tin.
6. Use the rolling pin to pick the pastry up and lay it over the tin. Gently press the pastry into the tin so that it fills all the contours. Be careful not to stretch the pastry or it will tear, or shrink back in the oven. Return it to the fridge for another 30 minutes, or more if the pastry still feels soft. Reserve the scraps for the trellis top.
7. Add the prepared apple filling (see recipe below), ensuring that the tart is full to 1 cm from the top.
8. On a lightly floured workbench roll out the remaining pastry to approximately 3 mm in thickness and at least 25 cm in width. Repeat if necessary.
9. Cut the dough into 5–10 mm strips and lay each strip over the top of the tart to give an attractive lattice effect. Trim off any excess from the edges.
10. Place directly into a preheated oven set at 195°C and bake for 40 minutes or until golden brown.
11. Allow to cool for 45 minutes before removing from the tin. Leave the base on the tart as this makes it easier to handle. Place on a wire cooling rack.
12. Using a pastry brush glaze the lattice top with apricot glaze (see recipe opposite).

Apple Filling

1. Once you have prepared the apples place them in a bowl of cold water with lemon juice in it. This prevents the apples from going brown while you are preparing the rest of the filling. Drain and dry well before combining with the other ingredients.
2. Mix the remaining ingredients with the apples.
3. Place in a bowl until required, but this filling should not be kept for days.

Custard

1. In a saucepan place the first amount of milk and sugar. Stir and bring to the boil.
2. Mix the second amount of milk with the custard powder in a bowl.
3. Add the boiled milk to the custard mix, then pour into the saucepan and return to a medium heat to thicken.
4. Cool before use.

Apricot Glaze

1. Mix the apricot jam and water together in a saucepan.
2. Bring to the boil, but do not boil too long as this will evaporate the water.
3. Once boiled pass through a sieve to remove any lumps or coarse apricot pulp.
4. Use while hot. You may need to warm the glaze from time to time.

Note: the consistency of the glaze can be adjusted with water.

Baileys Chocolate Truffles

These moreish truffles will be a favourite with young and old. Take care to read the notes on chocolate before starting as chocolate work is a very precise art. Imported chocolate can be purchased from specialty food stores and kitchen shops.

250 g fine milk chocolate
250 g white chocolate
200 ml fresh cream
50 g unsalted butter
25 g liquid glucose
25 ml Baileys liqueur
icing sugar – to powder hands
300 g melted tempered milk or white chocolate – for rolling truffles in

1. Break both types of chocolate into small pieces and set aside.
2. Place the fresh cream, butter and glucose in a heavy bottomed saucepan and heat until 90°C or just below boiling point.
3. Remove from the heat and add the broken chocolate, stirring until the chocolate has melted.
4. Pour the truffle mix into a baking tin lined with greaseproof paper (the size of the tin is not important, however, a 20 cm square tin is recommended).
5. Leave to set for approximately 8 hours in a cool place (not the refrigerator).
6. Cut into 2 cm squares with a sharp knife. Remove any greaseproof paper at this stage.
7. Using the icing sugar, powder the palms of your hands and roll the squares into even, round balls.
8. Place the balls onto a sheet of greaseproof paper and leave to set for a further 8 hours in a cool place.
9. Using the melted tempered milk or white chocolate (see notes on tempering chocolate below), cover your hands with chocolate and roll the balls in the chocolate, ensuring that you obtain an even, thin covering of chocolate around the balls. Alternatively, place the balls onto a chocolate dipping fork and dip into the melted chocolate. Tap to remove excess chocolate. Repeat until all the truffles have been covered in chocolate.
10. Place the truffles back onto the greaseproof paper to set.
11. Store in a cool dark place. Always serve truffles at room temperature.

Tempering Chocolate Coverture

This is an important procedure if you are using chocolate coverture.

1. Half fill a saucepan with cold water, bring to the boil, turn off the heat and remove the saucepan from the heat.
2. Break the chocolate into small pieces and place in a stainless steel bowl that will fit inside the saucepan of water. Place the bowl of chocolate in the hot water. Never allow any water to come into contact with the chocolate as this will cause the chocolate to thicken.
3. Stir the chocolate with a clean wooden spoon until it has reached 40°C and the chocolate has melted. You may need to remove the bowl from the water from time to time to avoid overheating the chocolate.
4. Tip two-thirds of the chocolate onto a marble slab or cold, clean work surface and using two palette knives rotate the chocolate until the chocolate has cooled to 27°C.
5. Place the cooled chocolate with the other third and mix thoroughly until well combined.

6. Place the bowl back onto the warm water and warm the chocolate coverture to exactly 30°C. Always use at this temperature and you will achieve a nice sheen on the chocolate once it has set.

Melting Chocolate Compound

You can use chocolate compounds which do not need to be tempered but the quality is inferior. Chocolate compounds only require melting and usually have a higher melting point.

1. Half fill a saucepan with cold water, bring to the boil, turn off the heat and remove the saucepan from the heat.
2. Break the chocolate into small pieces and place in a stainless steel bowl that will fit inside the saucepan of water. Place the bowl of chocolate in the hot water. Never allow any water to come into contact with the chocolate as this will cause the chocolate to thicken.
3. Stir the chocolate with a clean wooden spoon until it has reached 40°C and the chocolate has melted. You may need to remove the bowl from the water from time to time to avoid overheating the chocolate.
4. Use chocolate compound at 40°C to achieve a nice sheen once the chocolate has set.

KAY THOMPSON & MICHELLE WILSON

ROCKET KITCHEN

*T*he *'ultimate food with attitude' is how Kay Thompson and Michelle Wilson (below) describe the endless stream of food that comes from their busy kitchens. Kay moved from her position as head pastry chef at Pandoro Bakery to bake wholesale cakes in a small private hotel in Remuera. Her technical expertise needed business guidance so Michelle, who has the passion for driving the business, joined her in 1994 and the Rocket Kitchen was born in 1996.*

It has been a very creative bakery, with a superb range of cakes and, latterly, savoury items, all baked with top notch ingredients. Aimed at the wholesale market, their primary showcase is a very busy retail operation on Ponsonby Road, Auckland, and a catering kitchen which is attracting discerning clients. The main bakery is in Panmure, where they test bake and develop new lines and bake for their wholesale customers. Rocket Kitchen produces thoroughly modern food, beautifully presented and full of flavour.

Kay and Michelle have an excellent business plan with a goal to expand into frozen lines, to recognise the skills of their employees, and to build on their success.

Limoncello and Strawberry Torte

This torte is made moist and memorable with the Limoncello syrup. Limoncello is a strong but delicious liqueur with a really distinctive lemon flavour. It is made in Italy and is available from specialty food and liquor stores.

Limoncello Syrup

1. Heat the sugar and water in a saucepan and boil for 5 minutes.
2. Remove from the heat and add the Limoncello liqueur and lemon juice.
3. Cool before soaking the sponge fingers.

Filling

1. In a small bowl dissolve the gelatine in the hot water (keep warm to avoid setting).
2. Place the eggs and sugar in a stainless steel bowl and using a hand whisk, whisk over a saucepan of simmering water until the egg and sugar mixture is warm.
3. Pour the mixture into a mixing bowl fitted with a whisk and whisk until cold and the mixture has reached the ribbon stage (see the All About Cakes section).
4. In a large bowl lightly mix the mascarpone then fold in the egg and sugar mixture, one third at a time.
5. Lastly fold through the melted gelatine.
6. Place a layer of sponge fingers in a loose bottomed 23 cm round cake tin. You will need to cut them to fit (or use a disc of plain sponge instead of the sponge fingers).
7. Using a pastry brush lightly brush the sponge fingers with the Limoncello syrup.
8. Slice the strawberries in half and place around the inside of the cake tin (with their insides facing outwards).
9. Pour half the mascarpone filling over the sponge fingers and spread evenly.
10. Spread thinly sliced strawberries over the filling.
11. Place another layer of sponge fingers on top of the strawberries (or use a disc of plain sponge). Lightly brush with Limoncello syrup.
12. Pour the remaining mascarpone filling over the sponge fingers and spread evenly.
13. Decorate with flaked or grated white chocolate.
14. Refrigerate and allow to set overnight.
15. Remove from the cake tin by placing a hot, wet tea towel around the outside of the tin for a few minutes, then place the cake tin on a small, upside-down bowl and allow the tin to fall away, leaving you with the torte on the cake tin base.
16. Decorate by planting pineapple leaves in the top of the torte or by lightly dusting the white chocolate with cocoa powder and placing fresh strawberries on the top.

SYRUP
300 g granulated sugar
300 ml water
75 ml Limoncello liqueur
125 ml lemon juice

FILLING
10 g gelatine
250 ml hot water
220 g egg
160 g caster sugar
500 g mascarpone
2 packets of Savoiardi sponge fingers
  (available from the supermarket) or 2
  discs of plain sponge
250 g fresh strawberries

GARNISH
flaked or grated white chocolate
fresh strawberries
cocoa

Orange and Pinenut Polenta Cake

This is quite a chunky cake, with a great flavour that comes from the yoghurt and orange. Choose a fine polenta or cornmeal, and use whichever fruits you like to decorate the top.

CAKE

450 g plain yoghurt

130 g polenta (or coarse cornmeal)

zest of one orange (zested on the large grate of the grater)

200 g softened butter

320 g caster sugar

$^1/_2$ tsp baking soda

300 g Champion or Elfin Self Rising Flour

275 g eggs ($5^1/_2$)

45 g roasted pinenuts

75 g raisins

TOPPING

250 g granulated sugar

150 ml water

1 cinnamon stick

5 star anise

lemon rind strips (made by peeling 1 lemon with a potato peeler)

Fruits:

3 glacé pineapple rings (cut into 8 pieces)

5 dried apricot halves

2 tablespoons crystallised ginger

2 dried figs (cut into quarters)

1. Place the yoghurt, polenta and orange zest in a bowl, mix together and stand for 2 hours, covered.
2. In a mixing bowl fitted with a beater, cream the butter and sugar until light and fluffy.
3. Add the egg over 5 small additions, beating well between each to avoid curdling.
4. Sieve the flour and baking soda and mix in the roasted pinenuts and raisins.
5. Fold the dry ingredient mix into the creamed mixture. Once three-quarters mixed add the yoghurt and continue to mix until the batter is smooth. Do not overmix at this stage.
6. Place into a 20 cm round cake tin lined with baking paper on the bottom and sides.
7. Place directly into a preheated oven set at 150°C and bake for 1 hour or until a cake skewer comes out clean.
8. Cool before tipping onto a cooling rack. Remove the baking paper.
9. Decorate the top with poached glacé fruits (see recipe below).

Poached Glacé Fruits

1. Place the sugar, water, cinnamon stick, star anise and lemon rind in a saucepan, heat on low until all the sugar has dissolved, then bring to the boil.
2. Reduce the heat to allow the sugar syrup to simmer.
3. Add the fruits and poach for 5 minutes.
4. Drain well and arrange on top of the cake.

Photo of recipe on back cover

Lime and White Chocolate Cheesecake

In this rich baked cheesecake the lime cuts through the sweetness of the chocolate, giving it a refreshing zing. If you haven't got a springform tin, be sure to bake the cake in a loose bottomed tin. The raspberries make this a spectacular dessert cake.

Base

1. Place the digestive biscuits in a plastic bag and using a rolling pin crush the biscuits until even crumbs are formed.
2. Place the butter in a bowl and melt in a microwave.
3. Mix the melted butter and crushed biscuits together.
4. Press into a 23 cm round loose base springform cake tin which has the sides lined with baking paper. Chill.

Filling

1. Place the cream cheese and sugar in a mixing bowl fitted with a beater. Beat until light and fluffy, scraping down the sides from time to time.
2. Place the cream and chocolate in a bowl and microwave on high for 4 minutes. Stir until the mixture becomes smooth.
3. Mix the lime zest and juice with the cream cheese until smooth.
4. Then add the eggs slowly, mixing until smooth.
5. Lastly add the cream and chocolate and gently mix in until smooth.
6. Remove the crushed biscuit base-lined tin from the refrigerator and pour in the mixture. Smooth out the top if required.
7. Place directly into a preheated oven set at 120°C and bake for 1 hour or until the mixture has just set.
8. Remove from the oven and cool.
9. Loosen the springform tin and remove the cheesecake. Carefully remove the baking paper.
10. Decorate with fresh raspberries, mint leaves and zested lemon and lime rind which has been poached in a simple sugar syrup (see recipe below).
11. Serve sliced with a raspberry coulis (see recipe below), fresh raspberries and freshly whipped cream.

Raspberry Coulis

1. Place the raspberries in a saucepan and bring to the boil, stirring to break up.
2. Rub the cooked raspberries through a fine sieve to remove all the seeds.
3. Add enough simple sugar syrup to obtain a smooth, but not too sweet, taste.
4. Finally add a few drops of lemon juice. Cool before serving.

BASE
250 g digestive biscuits (1 packet)
100 g melted butter

FILLING
750 g cream cheese
220 g caster sugar
150 ml fresh cream
150 g white chocolate
2 limes (zest and juice)
175 g eggs (3$\frac{1}{2}$)

COULIS
250 g fresh raspberries
simple sugar syrup (1 part sugar to 1 part water, boil until sugar dissolves)
lemon juice

Wild One (Raspberry Mud Cake)

Very aptly named, the Wild One will become an all-time favourite. The combination of chocolate and raspberries is almost unequalled and the presentation is stunning, too. The chocolate shards require a fair amount of skill, but they are well worth mastering.

CAKE
435 ml hot water
325 g softened butter
235 g granulated sugar
40 g cocoa powder
400 g dark chocolate buttons
140 g mashed raspberries
5 ml raspberry essence (optional)
175 g eggs (3$\frac{1}{2}$)
285 g Champion or Elfin Self Rising
    Flour

GANACHE
300 ml fresh cream
500 g dark chocolate buttons

SHARDS
375 g dark chocolate buttons
    (1 packet)
375 g white chocolate buttons
    (1 packet)

1. Place the hot water in a saucepan and bring to the boil.
2. Remove from the heat and add the butter, then set aside until just melted but still hot.
3. Combine the sugar, cocoa powder and chocolate in a mixing bowl fitted with a whisk.
4. Add the hot butter and water to the chocolate mixture. Whisk on medium speed until smooth.
5. Mix in the mashed raspberries and raspberry essence.
6. Add the eggs one at a time while mixing. Scrape down the sides of the mixing bowl.
7. Sieve the flour and add to the mixture. Whisk on low speed until the mixture is smooth.
8. Pour into a 23 cm round loose base cake tin which has the sides and bottom lined with baking paper.
9. Place directly into a preheated oven set at 150°C and bake for 1$\frac{1}{2}$ hours or until a cake skewer comes out clean.
10. Once cool remove from the cake tin and take off the baking paper. Allow to cool completely on a cooling rack.
11. Place a sheet of baking paper underneath the cooling rack, then slowly pour the ganache (see recipe below) over the cake, starting at the centre and moving towards the outside, ensuring that the cake is completely covered (you may need to use a palette knife).
12. Give the cooling rack a shake to allow the ganache to settle evenly on the cake.
13. Once the ganache has finished dripping, carefully lift the covered cake off the cooling rack and place onto a serving plate.
14. Using a wide-bladed, pointed knife pierce the top of the cake where you want to place the white chocolate shards (see opposite), then carefully insert the shards into the holes.
15. Before the ganache is completely set, place the dark chocolate shards around the outside of the cake.
16. Tie a wide ribbon around the outside of the dark chocolate shards.

Chocolate Ganache
1. Place the cream in a saucepan and bring to the boil.
2. Remove from the heat and add the chocolate buttons.
3. Stir using a wooden spoon until the buttons have melted.
4. Leave to rest in the saucepan to thicken to pouring consistency – this should take approximately 45 minutes.
5. Use as directed.

Creating the Chocolate Shards

1. Half fill a saucepan with cold water, bring to the boil, and remove the saucepan from the heat.
2. Break the dark and white chocolate buttons into small pieces and place in separate stainless steel bowls that will fit inside the saucepan of water (one bowl at a time). Place the bowl of dark chocolate in the hot water. Never allow any water to come into contact with the chocolate as this will cause the chocolate to thicken.
3. Stir the chocolate with a clean wooden spoon until it has reached 40°C and melted. You may need to remove the bowl from the water from time to time to avoid overheating the chocolate.
4. Use chocolate compound at 40°C to achieve a nice sheen once the chocolate has set.
5. Repeat for white chocolate.
6. When both chocolates have melted, spread a thin layer (2 mm) of each onto a large sheet of baking paper using a palette knife.
7. Allow to nearly set, then using a sharp knife cut into shards. For the dark chocolate shards keep them straight and for the white chocolate shards cut them in a wave-type pattern.
8. Wait until the cut chocolate shards have completely set then carefully remove them from the baking paper by sliding a palette knife under each shard. You may need to have a few extra shards to allow for breakage.

SYDENHAM BAKERY

*B*aking seems to be in this family's blood, for the Kuipers have three bakeries within 500 metres of each other in the Christchurch suburb of Sydenham. John Kuipers (below), father of six, grew up in Holland and, after spending his formative years learning the art of baking, came to New Zealand as an assisted immigrant in 1959. He worked very hard on arrival and saved enough to finance the purchase of the Sydenham Cake Kitchen.

John has never looked back, building up his business, despite a devastating fire (he found another bakery and reopened within 24 hours), to a point where it was 80 percent wholesale. It is mainly a retail business now. His family and staff are extremely hard-working and loyal, and Sydenham Bakery has won Baker of the Year once and came a very close second in other years.

Constantly searching for new ideas and product lines, John travels to Australia and Europe annually, and has assisted his sons into their own businesses. He treasures and still bakes some of the original recipes he brought with him from Holland, including the well-known speculaas biscuits on page 152.

Toffee Biscuits

Many bakeries have their own special version of these crisp treats. At Sydenham the toffee biscuits are particularly good. Take special care when cooking the sugar and water to toffee, as the sugar reaches a very high temperature before turning golden and should be kept well away from the skin.

1. Place the softened butter, sugar, vanilla and salt in a mixing bowl fitted with a beater.
2. Cream until fluffy and light in colour.
3. Add the warmed eggs and cream again. Avoid curdling the mixture.
4. Add half of the sieved flour and cream until light – at this stage the mixture must be light and soft.
5. Add the rest of the flour and mix through until almost combined.
6. Add the crushed toffee and mix through until all the ingredients are thoroughly combined and the mixture is still soft. Lastly add the water and mix in.
7. Place the mixture directly into a piping bag fitted with a plain piping tube (tube diameter approximately 15 cm).
8. Pipe bulbs of mixture (approximately the size of a 20 cent piece and 15 g in weight) directly onto a lightly greased or baking paper-lined baking tray. Pipe in staggered rows allowing 3–4 cm between each biscuit. Sizes depend on individual requirements.
9. Place directly into a preheated oven set at 170°C and bake for 10–12 minutes or until the edges are a light, golden brown.
10. Allow to cool slightly and remove from the baking tray while still warm, otherwise the biscuits will stick and break upon removal.
11. Once cool wrap in cellophane bags and tie a gold ribbon around the top. A perfect gift.

190 g butter
190 g caster sugar
2–3 drops vanilla essence
pinch of salt
50 g egg (1), warmed
200 g Champion or Elfin Standard Plain Flour
20 ml water
110 g crushed toffee (see recipe below)

TOFFEE
200 g granulated sugar
50 ml cold water

Toffee

1. Place the sugar and water in a very clean, heavy bottomed saucepan.
2. Place on a high heat and boil until the water has evaporated and the toffee reaches a light, rich, golden caramel colour (150°C).
3. Remove from the heat and pour directly onto a lightly greased or baking paper-lined baking tray.
4. When cool break up the toffee and store in an airtight container until required for use. To crush the toffee place in a plastic bag and gently crush with a rolling pin. Avoid crushing the toffee too finely as this will result in a powder rather than even-sized pieces or nibs; if the toffee pieces are too large the toffee will not go through the piping nozzle.
5. Toss lightly in flour to keep the pieces separate.

Petite Christmas Fruit Mince Tarts

Baking really comes into its own at festive times in most cultures. No Christmas would be complete without a tinful of rich little fruity mince pies to serve to guests or after the traditional family feast.

PASTRY

170 g salted butter

85 g sugar

50 g egg (1)

260 g Champion or Elfin Standard
  Plain Flour

FILLING

250 g currants

250 g sultanas

200 g apple sauce

180 g suet

150 g soft brown sugar

150 g mixed peel

100 ml sherry

5 g salt

5 g mixed spice

5 g nutmeg

$^1/_4$ of a lemon (washed)

Sweet Pastry Base

1. Lightly cream the butter and sugar in a mixing bowl fitted with a beater or beat in a bowl with a wooden spoon.
2. Add the egg and mix until combined.
3. Lastly add the flour and mix to a paste. Only mix until the paste comes clean off the bowl. Be careful not to overmix or the pastry will become too elastic and doughy.
4. Transfer to a bowl. Cover and refrigerate for 30 minutes or overnight.
5. On a lightly floured workbench roll the pastry out into a sheet about 3 mm thick.
6. Using a 6.5 cm round cutter, cut out 24 bases and line the mini muffin tins. Gently press the pastry inside the tins and avoid any cracking around the bases.
7. Using a flower or star-shaped cutter cut 24 tops from the remaining rolled pastry, and set aside. Reserve any pastry scraps.
8. Place prepared Christmas mince filling (see recipe below) into a piping bag fitted with a large plain piping tube and pipe approximately 20 g into each pastry lined case. Alternatively, fill each pastry lined case with a teaspoon of filling.
9. Lightly brush or spray the edges of the pastry cases with water.
10. Place the round tops over the filling, pressing slightly around the edges to seal the tops to the bottom or place the sweet pastry star shape in the middle of the filling.
11. If desired, lightly glaze the tops with egg wash.
12. Place directly into a preheated oven set at 180°C and bake for 15 minutes or until light golden brown.
13. If desired, immediately sprinkle with caster sugar upon exiting the oven.
14. Allow to cool, remove from their tins and store in an airtight container.

Christmas Mince Filling

1. Put all the ingredients through a mincer or finely chop ensuring that all the ingredients are well combined.
2. Place in a clean airtight container and seal.
3. Refrigerate for up to 2 weeks before using.

Speculaas Biscuits

Speculaas biscuits are a traditional Dutch crispy biscuit with a great spice aroma that make an ideal special occasion gift. They are shaped with a special wooden mould and baked on a layer of very fine flaked almonds.

100 g white biscuit crumbs
  (Vanilla Wines)
80 ml milk
180 g butter
good pinch of salt
290 g soft brown sugar
400 g Champion or Elfin Standard
  Plain Flour
10 g speculaas spices (see recipe below)
10 g baking soda
blanched flaked almonds

SPICES
20 g cinnamon
15 g mixed spice
5 g ground ginger
5 g ground nutmeg
5 g ground cardamom

1. Place the biscuit crumbs and milk in a small bowl. Using a wooden spoon mix together to form a paste. Place aside.
2. Place the butter, salt and sugar in a mixing bowl fitted with a beater and blend on low speed until mixed together. Do not cream the mixture.
3. Add the biscuit paste and mix through until combined.
4. Sieve the flour, speculaas spices (see recipe below) and baking soda together. Add to the butter and sugar mixture and mix on a low speed until a firm dough has been formed.
5. Place the dough in a plastic bag or wrap in plastic wrap and then place in the refrigerator overnight. This will allow the spices to develop their flavours.
6. Remove the dough from the refrigerator at least $1\frac{1}{2}$ hours before you require it. Work the dough by continuous moulding with your hands until soft but firm to work with.
7. Roll the dough out to a thickness of 3–4 mm and, using a round, 5 cm diameter biscuit cutter, cut into discs or press the dough into a special speculaas biscuit mould (see Sources, page 162), then trim the edges.
8. Sprinkle a lightly greased or baking paper-lined baking tray with the flaked almonds and place the cut out biscuits on top.
9. Place directly into a preheated oven set at 170°C and bake for 12–15 minutes until golden brown and firm to touch.
10. Remove from the baking tray once cool and repeat the baking process.
11. Once cool store in an airtight container.

Note: the almonds can be reused time after time to avoid wastage.

Speculaas Spices
Mix all the spices together thoroughly and store in an airtight container until required.

GLYN ABBOTT

UNDER THE RED VERANDAH

*B*aker Glyn Abbott (below) and artist Roger Hickin have lovingly restored an historic homestead and corner store in the Christchurch suburb of Linwood, and now operate a bakery, café and gallery on the street level of this handsome property. A calm, relaxing atmosphere within to showcase Glyn's deliciously healthy baking is appreciated by a steady stream of customers who come from near and far to sip coffee, purchase organic breads and view the artwork.

Glyn is committed to sourcing organic ingredients, and the fare is wholesome and delicious. Tasting is of paramount importance to this baker, and she has surrounded herself in the generously staffed kitchen with cooks and bakers who all have great palates. It is a relaxed, happy environment where customers can linger over breakfast, lunch and snacks.

Organic Focaccia

Focaccia has become a mainstream bread in the past few years. It is ideal to have on hand for serving with dips and spreads, or simply to split and fill with salad and a variety of vegetables, generously drizzled with a tasty dressing. Try toasting in chunks and serving with extra virgin olive oil.

1. Combine the honey with 125 ml of the water and sprinkle in the yeast. Stir and leave until the yeast begins to bubble, approximately 10 minutes.
2. Place the flour and salt onto your work surface. Make a well and add the balance of the water and yeast mixture.
3. Mix or knead the dough by hand using the technique shown in the All About Bread section. Continue kneading until the ingredients are well combined. This final kneading should take about 10–15 minutes (check if you have fully developed the dough by using the stretch test).
4. Place the dough in a lightly oiled bowl large enough to allow the dough to double in bulk. Cover with plastic and leave in a warmish place (23–25°C) until the dough has truly doubled in size (approximately 40 minutes).
5. Gently knock back the dough in the bowl. This will deflate it slightly, but will develop more strength. Cover again and leave for another 15–20 minutes.
6. Tip the dough out onto a lightly floured bench, being gentle with the dough; do not aggressively punch it down, or squeeze all the gas from within. Pick the dough piece up and gently tuck the edges underneath, pulling the surface tight around the mass to form a ball shape. Lay the pieces back on the floured bench and cover with a proofing cloth (or tea towel). Give an intermediate proof of 10 minutes.
7. Uncover the dough and flatten or roll to the size of a round dinner plate (approximately 25 cm in diameter). Place onto a greased or baking paper lined baking tray.
8. Final proof for 15–20 minutes. Cover with lightly oiled plastic to prevent skinning and chilling of the dough.
9. Gently brush the top surface with lots of olive oil, then using your fingertips gently dimple the dough several times to allow even rising when the focaccia is baking.
10. Sprinkle with freshly chopped rosemary or sage and rock salt or flaked salt.
11. Place into a preheated oven set at 200°C and bake for 20–25 minutes. Do not overbake.
12. Place the baked focaccia onto a wire cooling rack and immediately brush again with olive oil if desired.

Note: the organic flour can be replaced with Champion or Elfin High Grade Flour and Champion or Elfin Wholemeal Flour, however, you may have to adjust the water level to obtain the correct dough consistency.

BREAD
25 g honey
250 ml water
$^1/_2$ tablespoon Elfin Dried Yeast
500 g organic white flour
5 g salt

TOPPINGS
olive oil
fresh rosemary or sage
rock salt or flaked salt
sliced olives (optional)

Organic Nine Grain Bread

Honey is used to raise the yeast and imparts a subtle flavour to this wholesome loaf. This is a very popular loaf with Glyn's regular customers and will keep fresh for several days. Excellent for toasting, too.

GRAIN MIXTURE

15 g kibbled wheat

15 g kibbled rye

15 g coarsely ground corn grits or polenta

15 g whole brown rice

15 g rolled oats

15 g hulled millet

15 g pearl barley

15 g sunflower seeds

15 g linseed

75 ml hot water

DOUGH

15 g honey

180 ml water

8 g Elfin Dried Yeast (1 sachet)

150 g organic white flour

150 g organic wholemeal flour

soaked grain mixture from above

5 g salt

Finished dough temperature: 28°C

GLAZE

15 g honey

10 ml hot water

Grain Mixture

1. Place all of the grains together in a bowl and mix to combine.
2. Add the hot water. Using a wooden spoon mix together.
3. Cover and soak for 8 hours or overnight.

Dough

1. Combine the honey with the water and sprinkle in the yeast. Leave until the yeast begins to bubble – approximately 10 minutes.
2. Place the white flour, wholemeal flour, soaked grain and salt onto your work surface. Make a well and add the water and yeast mixture.
3. Mix or knead the dough by hand using the technique shown in the All About Bread section. Continue kneading until the ingredients are well combined. This final kneading should take about 10–15 minutes (check if you have fully developed the dough by using the stretch test).
4. Place the dough in a lightly oiled bowl large enough to allow the dough to double in bulk. Cover with plastic and leave in a warmish place (23–25°C) until the dough has truly doubled in size – approximately $1\frac{1}{2}$ hours.
5. Gently knock back the dough in the bowl. This will deflate it slightly, but will develop more strength. Cover again and leave for 60 minutes.
6. Tip the dough out onto a lightly floured bench, being gentle with the dough; do not aggressively punch it down, or squeeze all the gas from within. Pick the dough piece up and gently tuck the edges underneath, pulling the surface tight around the mass to form a ball shape. Lay the pieces back on the floured bench and cover with a proofing cloth (or tea towel). Give an intermediate proof of 10 minutes. While you wait, lightly grease a bread baking tin (rectangle shape and large enough to hold a 700–800 g loaf, remembering that the finished baked loaf is small in volume and dense textured inside).
7. Uncover the dough and mould the dough piece into a vienna or baton shape. To achieve this flatten the dough piece out as for rolling up a swiss roll, then tightly roll the dough towards you as you would for a swiss roll, applying pressure with your hands as you roll – the tighter the roll the better.
8. Place the dough piece in the bread tin.
9. Final proof for approximately 1–$1\frac{1}{2}$ hours or until double in size. Cover with plastic to prevent skinning and chilling of the dough. Use the indentation test to tell when the dough is fully proofed.
10. Before you load the bread into the oven, spray water into the oven cavity. Close the door quickly so you don't lose any of the steam.
11. Place the tin directly into a preheated oven set at 220°C and bake for approximately 25–30 minutes (remember to tap the bottom of the loaf; if it sounds hollow it is baked).

12. Tip the bread out of the tin as soon as you remove it from the oven and brush with honey glaze immediately (see recipe below).
13. Cool on a wire rack.

Note: the organic flour can be replaced with Champion or Elfin High Grade Flour and Champion or Elfin Wholemeal Flour, however, you may have to adjust the water level to obtain the correct dough consistency.

Honey Glaze

Dissolve the honey in the hot water.

DAVID GRIFFITHS

VINNIES RESTAURANT

*P*assionate about food, David Griffiths (below) and his partner Prue Barton are completely uncompromising when it comes to fine ingredients and exceptional taste. Thus, the bread served in their restaurant, Vinnies, in the Auckland suburb of Herne Bay, is baked each day for evening diners.

David has a repertoire of loaves, but his pain au levain is the bread that most customers are knocked out by, for it has a dark crusty exterior and a dense moist crumb with tons of flavour. The starter is made from organic grapes which are fermented and give a tart sour taste to the bread.

Pain au Levain

So impressed was David Griffiths with the bread in San Francisco that he sourced this recipe from Chez Panisse, a world famous restaurant in Berkeley. He created his own starter and has kept it going for over seven years. The bread is a real winner when served with Vinnies' special dips.

The Starter

1. Place the flour and water in a non-porous mixing bowl.
2. Using a clean wooden spoon mix the ingredients together to form a light batter, beating well to incorporate as much air as possible.
3. Wrap the grapes or raisins in a muslin cloth and lightly crush. Tie the ends and leave a length of string at the end.
4. Suspend the muslin cloth full of grapes or raisins in the batter, cover the bowl with a muslin cloth and leave at room temperature (22–24°C) for 7–8 days.
5. Check every second day to ensure the batter has not become too runny. If the batter is too runny, add one part water and one part flour to bring it back to its original consistency.
6. After 7–8 days remove the muslin full of grapes or raisins and discard. The batter should have fermented and be slightly sour when sniffed. Now you are ready to build your starter.

Building the Starter Dough

1. Remove the muslin cloth from the top of the bowl and mix in 125 ml of the filtered water (25°C) to the fermented batter. Beat well using a clean wooden spoon.
2. Then add two parts of organic whole-wheat flour and one part organic rye flour (this amount will vary but ensure that you keep to the two parts of organic whole-wheat flour and one part organic rye flour).
3. Mix until you have formed a firm dough; you may have to knead the dough by hand if the dough becomes too hard to mix with the wooden spoon (knead only until the dough has come together, 2–3 minutes).
4. Place back in a lightly oiled bowl, cover and leave at room temperature for 4 hours, then refrigerate for 2 days before using.

Maintaining the Starter Dough

At the end of day two (in the evening)

1. In a large mixing bowl break down the starter with the water, then mix in the flours (this can be done either by hand or wooden spoon).
2. Cover loosely and leave at room temperature for 3 hours, then refrigerate overnight.
3. The starter dough must be refreshed every 3–4 days by breaking down with 250 ml of filtered water (25°C) and reforming with two parts of organic whole-wheat flour and one part organic rye flour (this amount will vary but ensure that you keep to the two parts of organic whole-wheat flour and one part organic rye flour).

STARTER
250 g organic flour
250 ml filtered or still mineral water (25°C)
340 g organic grapes or organic raisins

DAY 7/8
450 g starter dough (from above)
1 litres filtered water (25°C)
300 g Champion or Elfin High Grade Flour
300 g organic whole-wheat flour

DAY 9/10
500 g Champion or Elfin High Grade Flour
200 g organic whole-wheat flour
100 g organic rye flour
25 g sea salt

Final dough temperature 27–29°C

4. Place back into a lightly oiled bowl, cover and leave at room temperature for 4 hours, then refrigerate overnight or until ready to use.

Making the Bread Dough

The next day, add 250 ml of filtered water (25°C) to the starter dough and do the following:

1. Mix the dry ingredients together then knead the flours into the starter dough.
2. Turn the dough out onto a very lightly floured work surface and knead by hand until you have fully developed the dough. Check by using the 'stretch test', explained in the All About Bread section (if using a mixer avoid overmixing as this will result in a sticky dough). Check the final dough temperature as this will determine how fast the dough will take to double in size.
3. Once you have achieved full dough development, place the dough into a lightly oiled bowl until doubled in size. This can take 2–4 hours depending on the temperature of the room.
4. Once the dough has doubled in size gently place the dough onto a lightly floured work surface and gently knock back the dough to expel all the gases.
5. Divide the dough into two even-sized pieces.
6. Mould into a round ball shape by cupping your hands around the dough and moving in a circular motion, pulling the skin tight over the dough. Don't overdo it though, or the skin will rip and this will spoil the appearance of the finished product. The final shape will look like a smooth ball, but with a rough, scrunched-up bottom. This is called the seam. When the shaping is complete, place the bread dough onto a baking tray lightly dusted with semolina or polenta. Cover the baking tray with plastic or a proofing cloth, and leave in a warm, draught-free place, to rise.
7. Final proof for approximately $1\frac{1}{2}$–2 hours. Cover with plastic to prevent skinning and chilling of the dough. Use the indentation test to tell when the dough is fully proofed.
8. The oven should be preheated to 250°C, with a baking stone in place and a small tray of water in the bottom to create steam. Gently transfer one loaf by sliding onto a baker's peel lightly dusted with semolina or polenta. (If you do not have a baking stone you can leave the bread dough on the baking tray.)
9. Using a sieve dust the loaves with rye flour and, using a razor blade or sharp knife, score the top of the loaf in a decorative trellis pattern.
10. Just before you load the bread into the oven, spray water into the oven cavity. Close the door quickly so you don't lose any of the steam.
11. With the peel and loaf in one hand, open the oven with the other, and gently 'flick' the loaf off the peel and onto the baking stone (or place the baking tray directly into the oven). Close the oven door immediately.
12. Turn the heat down to 200°C and bake for 50 minutes, checking the loaves for even baking. If necessary, turn them around.
13. Cool on a wire rack before cutting and eating them with the following dips.

Eggplant Dip

This dip will keep for a day or two, and is perfect for spreading on bread or crackers.

1. Pierce the eggplant several times with a sharp knife and place in a small roasting pan with the whole garlic bulb. Roast in a preheated oven set at 280°C for 45 minutes, turning every 10 minutes.
2. Remove the skins from the eggplant and garlic bulb while still hot.
3. Place the eggplant and garlic cloves in a food processor and blend until roughly pureed.
4. With the food processor still blending, add the lemon juice and olive oil slowly until a smooth purée has been formed.
5. Season with freshly ground salt and pepper to taste.
6. Remove from the blender and place into serving bowls. Cover and chill in the refrigerator until required.

1 large eggplant
1 whole garlic bulb
juice of 1 lemon
135 g olive oil
salt and pepper to taste

Brandade Dip

A popular dip that is reminiscent of the flavours of the Mediterranean.

1. Rub the cod fillets with the rock salt, coating both sides. Cover and leave overnight in the refrigerator.
2. Rinse the cod fillets with cold water and soak in cold water for 12 hours.
3. Peel and dice the potato, place into a saucepan with the milk, thyme and garlic cloves. Bring to the boil.
4. Add the drained cod fillets and poach until the potato and cod are cooked.
5. Remove the thyme sprig and place the cod, potato and garlic in a food processor. Blend until a smooth purée is formed.
6. Slowly add the milk until the mixture just holds it shape (the mixture will thicken slightly upon standing).
7. Add the olive oil and blend in.
8. Season with freshly ground salt and pepper to taste.
9. Remove from the blender and place into serving bowls. Cover and chill in the refrigerator until required.

150 g blue cod fillets (skinned and boned)
350 g rock salt
1 small potato
200 ml milk
1 sprig of thyme
2 cloves of garlic (peeled)
20 g olive oil
salt and pepper to taste

SOURCES

The following shops and establishments stock specialist baking/cooking equipment and ingredients:

THE EPICUREAN WORKSHOP
6 Morrow Street
Newmarket
Auckland
Phone   (09) 524 0906
Fax   (09) 524 2017
Call Free   0800 555 151

MILLY'S KITCHEN SHOP
273 Ponsonby Road
Ponsonby
Auckland
Phone   (09) 376 1550
Fax   (09) 360 1520
Call Free   0800 200 123
Fax Free   0800 200 246

MOORE WILSON
Cnr Tory and College Streets
Wellington
Phone   (04) 384 9906
Fax   (04) 382 9263

CHAMPION AND ELFIN FLOUR, DRIED YEAST AND EDMONDS PRODUCTS
Retail   – all major Supermarket retailers
Commercial Flour, etc.   – Champion Call Free   0800 11 0800

NEW ZEALAND BIO GRAINS LIMITED
35 Dobson Street West
Ashburton
Phone   (03) 308 7349
Fax   (03) 307 0092

BIBLIOGRAPHY

Reinhart, Peter *Crust & Crumb*. California: Ten Speed Press, 1998.

Ortiz, Joe *The Village Baker*. California: Ten Speed Press, 1993.

Field, Carol *The Italian Baker*. New York: Harper and Row, 1985.

Silverton, Nancy *Breads from the La Brea Bakery*. New York: Villard Books, 1996.

Connelly, Paul and Pittam, Malcolm *Practical Bakery*. London: Hodder & Stoughton, 1997.

Gisslen, Wayne *Professional Baking*. New York: John Wiley & Sons, Inc., 1985

Hanneman, L.J. *Patisserie*. London: Heinemann Professional Publishing Ltd, 1980.

Hanneman, L.J. *Bakery: Bread & Fermented Goods*. London: Heinemann Professional Publishing Ltd, 1980.

Roux, Michel and Albert *Patisserie*. London: Macdonald & Co (Publishers) Ltd, 1986.

Galli, Franco *The Il Fornaio Baking Book*. San Francisco: Chronicle Books, 1993.

INDEX OF INGREDIENTS, EQUIPMENT AND BASIC TECHNIQUES

ascorbic acid, 22

baker's peel, 26
baker's percentages, 30–1
baking powder, 18
baking stone, 27
baking tray/tins and moulds, 25
bicarbonate of soda, 19
biscuit cutter, 29
biscuits. *See* cakes, sponges and biscuits
bread makers, 24
bread making, 34–42
    baking guidelines, 41–2
    causes of faults, 42
    dough development, 38–41
    dough temperature, 36
    ingredients, 34
    processes, 34–5
    steps in mixing and kneading, 37
    steps in yeast-raised
        production, 35–6

cake decorating, 47–8
cakes, sponges and biscuits, 43–8
    baking guidelines, 46–7
    causes of faults, 48
    cooling, 47
    ingredients, 43–4
    mixing methods, 44–5
    points to consider, 46
chocolate compounds, 20
chocolate coverture, 20
choux pastry, 55–6
cocoa, 19
cooling rack, 27
cream of tartar, 18

dough conditioners, 22
dough development, 38–41
dough scraper or cutter, 23
dough slashing knife, 26
dough temperature, 31–2, 36

eggs, 15–16

fats, 17–18
fine mesh sieve, 26
food flavours, 22
formulas, 30–2
freezer, 26
fruits, 19

gluten, 11

knives
    dough slashing knife, 26
    palette knife, 29
    serrated knife, 28

measurements, 30–2
measuring cups and spoons, 29
melting chocolate, 20
metric conversions, 31–2
milk and milk products, 16–17
mixer, 23–4
mixing bowl, 24

nuts, 19

oils, 17–18
oven, 27

palette knife, 29
pastries, 49–57
    causes of faults, 57
    choux pastry, 55–6
    ingredients, 49–51
    mixing and processing
        methods, 51–6
    puff pastry, 51–3
    short pastry, 53–5
    sweet pastry, 53–5
pastry bag, 28
pastry brush, 28
pastry cutter, 29
pastry docker, 28
pastry sheeter, 28
pastry wheel, 29
piping tube, 28

plant mister, 27
proofing basket, 24
proofing cabinet, 25
proofing cloth, 24
puff pastry, 51–3

razor blade, 26
recipe balance, 30
refrigerator, 25
roller milling, 11
rolling pin, 28

salt, 14
scales, 23
scaling ingredients, 30
scissors, 26
serrated knife, 28
short pastry, 53–5
sieve, 26
spices, 20
sponges. *See* cakes, sponges and biscuits

spray bottle, 27
stone milling, 10
sugar, 14–15
sweet pastry, 53–5

thermometer, 23

water, 21
water temperature, 31–2
wheat flour
    composition, 11
    extraction rate, 11
    gluten, 11
    milling, 10–11
    storage, 12
    strength, 11, 12
    types, 12–14

yeast, 20–1
your hands, 23

INDEX OF RECIPES

almond round, 135
apple tart, 138–9
authentic bagels, 87

bagels, 87
baguettes, 64–5
Baileys chocolate truffles, 140–1
biscuits
    almond round, 135
    chocolate hazelnut pretzels, 107
    dream biscuits, 75
    speculaas biscuits, 152
    toffee biscuits, 149
Black Forest gateau, 105–6
boiled festive fruit cake, 115
boules, 64–5
brandade dip, 161
breads
    baguettes, 64–5
    boules, 64–5
    brioches, 59
    caraway rye bread, 89–90
    ciabatta, 80–2
    croissants, 60
    Dovedale gluten-free rice-millet bread, 94
    Dovedale rye and linseed, 93
    olive bread, 130–1
    organic focaccia, 154
    organic nine grain bread, 156–7
    organic sourdough bread, 125–6
    pane italiano, 127–8
    panettone, 132–3
brioches, 59

cakes
    almond round, 135
    Black Forest gateau, 105–6
    boiled festive fruit cake, 115
    carrot cake, 68
    Greek coconut cake, 67
    honey roll, 98
    Mediterranean orange cake, 119
    orange and pinenut polenta cake, 144

    Wild One (raspberry mud cake), 146–7
caramel petits fours, 103
caraway rye bread, 89–90
carrot cake, 68
cheesecake
    German baked cheesecake, 116
    lime and white chocolate cheesecake, 145
chicken, cranberry and brie pie, 102
chocolate coverture, 140–1
chocolate ecstasy muffins, 111
chocolate hazelnut pretzels, 107
ciabatta, 80–2
citron tart, 120
coconut cake, 67
crackers, cracked pepper and Parmesan, 79
croissants, 60

Danish pastries, 73–4
deluxe shortbread, 97
dessert pizza, 83–4
dips, 161
Dovedale gluten-free rice-millet bread, 94
Dovedale rye and linseed, 93
dream biscuits, 75
Dutch apricot flan, 108–9

eggplant dip, 161

flan, Dutch apricot, 108–9
focaccia, 154
fruit cake, 115
fruit mince tarts, 150
fruit tart, 70

German baked cheesecake, 116
Gevulde Koeken, 135
Greek coconut cake, 67

honey and almond tart, 76
honey roll, 98

leavens
   Dovedale leaven, 94
   pain au levain, 159–60
   pane acido, 122–4
lime and white chocolate
     cheesecake, 145
Limoncello and strawberry torte, 143

maple muffins (without egg), 112
Mediterranean orange cake, 119
mince tarts, 150
muffins, 111–12

olive bread, 130–1
Oma's Dutch apple tart, 138–9
onion jam, 131
orange and pinenut polenta cake, 144
orange cheesecake muffins, 111
organic focaccia, 154
organic nine grain bread, 156–7
organic sourdough bread, 125–6
organic sourdough starter (pane
     acido), 122–4

pain au levain, 159–60
pane acido (organic sourdough
     starter), 122–4
pane italiano, 127–8
panettone, 132–3
Paris Brest, 62–3
pastries
   Danish pastries, 73–4
   Paris Brest, 62–3

pâté à pain, 64–5
petite Chistmas fruit mince tarts, 150
pies
   chicken, cranberry and brie pie, 102
   steak, caramelised onion and red
     pepper mustard pie, 101
pizza, dessert, 83–4

raspberry mud cake (Wild One), 146–7

shortbread, 97
speculaas biscuits, 152
spinach and parmesan muffins, 112
steak, caramelised onion and red
     pepper mustard pie, 101
stollen, 136–7
summer fruit tart, 70

tarts
   caramel petits fours, 103
   citron tart, 120
   honey and almond tart, 76
   Oma's Dutch apple tart, 138–9
   petite Chistmas fruit mince
     tarts, 150
   summer fruit tart, 70
toffee biscuits, 149
torte, Limoncello and strawberry, 143
truffles, Baileys chocolate, 140–1

Wild One (raspberry mud cake), 146–7